grown boys

JAMES B. HALL, M.D.

grown boys

7 BABY STEPS TO MANHOOD FOR A FATHERLESS GENERATION

www.grownboys.com

ISBN: 979-8-9939729-0-9 (paperback)
ISBN: 979-8-9939729-1-6 (ebook)
ISBN: 979-8-9939729-2-3 (hardcover)
ISBN: 979-8-9939729-3-0 (audiobook)

Printed in: Brookhaven, MS, United States of America

Library of Congress Control Number: 2026901133

Ordering Information:
Special discounts are available on quantity purchases by corporations, associations, and others. For details, contact grownboys@anointedneph.com

Publisher's Cataloging-in-Publication Data

Names: Hall, James Bernard, author.
Title: Grown boys : 7 baby steps to manhood for a fatherless generation / James Bernard Hall.
Description: Brookhaven, MS : Jamerl Publishing, 2026.
Identifiers: LCCN 2026901133 (print) | ISBN 979-8-9939-729-0-9 (paperback) | ISBN 979-8-9939-729-2-3 (hardcover) | ISBN 979-8-9939-729-1-6 (ebook) | ISBN 979-8-9939-729-3-0 (audiobook)
Subjects: LCSH: Fatherless families. | Men--Family relationships. | Men--Social conditions. | Masculinity. | Self-help techniques. | BISAC: FAMILY & RELATIONSHIPS / General. | SOCIAL SCIENCE / Men's Studies.
Classification: LCC HQ756 H35 2026 (print) | LCC HQ756 (ebook) | DDC 306.8742--dc23.

Dedication

To the many fatherless young men, and to the many parents, coaches, pastors, teachers, mentors, and big brothers fighting to end the fallout of a fatherless society

Table of Contents

INTRODUCTION

Proclaim ye this among the Gentiles; Prepare war, ***wake up the mighty men****, let all the men of war draw near; let them come up.*
— Joel 3:9, emphasis added (KJV)

We have a new pandemic—not a new strain of COVID this time, but a pandemic of fatherlessness. This disease does not cause severe physical illness in 5% of the population like COVID[1]. Instead, it affects 100% of the population! And if you have not encountered its effects, you will soon.

As a result of this disease, your family legacy may even terminate after several generations. Fatherlessness has weakened every sector of society, and it is like terminal cancer in today's world. But if we can wake up the mighty men, we can win the war on the family. History teaches us that strong men create strong families, which in turn create strong communities and nations. If we can put men back in their rightful place, we can quickly solve most of our societal ills. The modern pandemic is not tuberculosis, black plague, scurvy, or malaria—it is a pandemic of grown boys.

---

1 Sheldon H. Preskorn, "The 5% of the Population at High Risk for Severe COVID-19 Infection Is Identifiable and Needs to Be Taken Into Account When Reopening the Economy." *Journal of Psychiatric Practice* 26, no. 3 (2020), 219–27, https://doi.org/10.1097/PRA.0000000000000475.

THE ELEPHANT IN THE ROOM

The good news is that we don't have to guess how this pandemic turns out. We've seen its impact in nature already.

How does fatherlessness affect the animal kingdom? Do we see the same sickness in the animal world that we see in the human world when there is a lack of fathers? The Delinquents of Pilanesberg, a story reported by CBS News in 1999, reveals the answer to this question.

In the 1990s, rhinos started to turn up dead in South Africa's Pilanesberg Park. According to the CBS coverage, "Thirty-nine rhinos, 10 percent of the population in the park, were killed."[2] The killings were not caused by poachers, even though that might have been the first assumption, and no horns were taken. No, during the investigation, the park rangers discovered that they had a gang of murdering psychopathic elephants. To be exact, young male elephants were killing the rhinos. *Why?* The young male elephants had no role models.

How did this happen? Approximately 20 years prior to this mass rhino killing, Kruger National Park had too many elephants, so researchers decided to euthanize adult elephants and save the baby elephants, since the young elephants were easier to transport to other parks. Veterinarian Hym Ebedes, who had given the go-ahead for the relocations, said that the elephants might not adjust well, but there was no other option. Unfortunately, he was exactly right, and the animals did have difficulty adjusting.

The researchers had good intentions, but the outcome was not good. Years later, the orphan elephants became teens, and that's when the killing started at Pilanesberg Park. The elephants were noted to run in gangs,

---

2 "The Delinquents," CBS News, August 22, 2000, https://www.cbsnews.com/news/the-delinquents.

with one elephant leading each pack. The elephants also acted aggressively toward tourist vehicles.

Researchers decided to euthanize five of the elephants, since they could not send them to boot camp or juvenile reform school. However, the rhino killings continued. After studying the elephants for a while, the researchers discovered that these gangbanger elephants were suffering from *excess testosterone.*

The rangers decided to find role models for these juvenile elephants. They brought in large bull elephants. These older elephants established a hierarchy by "sparring with the younger elephants to discourage them from being sexually active."[3] This sparring lowered the testosterone level in the young elephants. Once the bull elephants arrived, rhino killings stopped immediately.

The moral of this story is to never disrupt what God has set in place. Fatherhood is critical to the animal kingdom, and even more so in the man kingdom.

WHAT FAMILY?

Without fathers, every kingdom suffers. The more intelligent you are, the more you need a father's presence to shape your mind and subdue a rogue mentality. A child with a rogue mentality feels like he is all alone—it is a "me against the world" approach to life. Adolescent bull elephants and adolescent boys share this common denominator in social dynamics.

Godly order was set up from the beginning when God made Adam first, as the foundation for all mankind. Adam, the first man according to Genesis 1:26–27, held the keys to leadership along the lines of family.

3 "The Delinquents."

Eve, Adam's wife, was taken from Adam's rib (Genesis 2:22–23), and she was designed to be his helper, his ride-or-die chick. But sadly, today, divine order has been misconstrued and challenged on all levels. God designed the family to be a representation of His spiritual family.

In 1 Corinthians 11:3, Paul says, "But I would have you know, that the head of every man is Christ; and the head of the woman is the man; and the head of Christ is God" (KJV). If you believe in God, then you must conclude that He designed everything the way He wanted it.

Modern thinking has challenged God by challenging the family structure. This challenge has caused many men to give up their roles as leaders of the family. In America, the home has been attacked, men have been attacked, stay-at-home women have been attacked, and every aspect of family life has been attacked.

Our adversary—the devil—wants to steal our kids, kill our ambitions, and destroy our dreams. He accomplishes this feat by hijacking our thinking so that we cannot comprehend godly order. He convinces women that they can head this corporation called family better than a husband/wife team could. The devil convinces men that they are no longer needed in the family. Even the government has intentionally—or unintentionally—removed men from the home in an attempt to end poverty. The definition of family has been tainted.

A family is composed of a man, a woman, and kids. A woman and kids do not compose a complete family, since the most critical element of this family is missing—the man. We will explore how we got here in chapter 2, as well as discuss the steps necessary to regain what has been lost. In chapter 4, we will discuss how weak men make weak families, weak communities, weak cities, and weak nations. If any country is weak, it is because the men are weak.

This book will discuss how the conspiracy to eliminate fathers from the home has allowed the enemy to create poverty, crime, mass shootings, and homelessness. We will discuss how a paradigm shift has taken place in our world with regard to what manhood really means. I am having a conversation in this book with community leaders, pastors, teachers, and coaches who recognize the problem but need concrete solutions. We will highlight these solutions so we can end the epidemic of fatherlessness and the social misfortunes associated with grown boys.

Someone must take responsibility for what is happening so that the buck stops with the men. And just like the delinquent elephants needed older bulls to straighten them out and show them how to behave, this generation of young men needs strong men to do the same.

ESCAPING THE TRAP

I am a nephrologist by career, but a father and minister by calling. Nephrologists manage chronic kidney disease, kidney failure, hypertension, and diabetes. Our clinic has scriptures on the wall to highlight how critically the spirit, soul, and body are connected to overall health. Having scriptures on the wall is somewhat unique, and the following scripture is in our lobby: "Beloved, I wish above all things that thou mayest prosper and be in health, even as thy soul prospereth," from 3 John 1:2 (KJV). Medicine is a ministry because anyone can write prescriptions, but it takes a physician to heal the whole person. My wife and I pray with patients, have Bible studies with them, bring them to church, and minister to their souls.

We live in a broken society, so people need more than pill pushers. Our trademarked company slogan is "Your health is the most important thing you own second to your soul!" We encourage a healthy body and a healthy soul because you do not want to lose either.

We believe that our life purpose is to help our community, so we mentor many young men and women. We have been shocked by the number of problems we encounter due to lack of fatherhood. I have noticed a massive difference in my success compared to the success of my fatherless relatives. We rode the same school buses, went to the same school, had the same teachers, and bear the same last name, but our paths diverged after high school simply because I had a father and they didn't. Our paths will probably never cross again.

I ask you, is the difference the government's fault or the dad's fault? Is it racism or their dad's fault? I am writing this book to destroy what's destroying us—the epidemic of fatherlessness. My goal is to get fathers back in the home, teach young men to get married before entering fatherhood, and celebrate the blessing of being a dad.

We've got to change our thinking so that we no longer assume manhood is signified by the presence of a penis and testes. A penis and testes only signify malehood, not manhood, and malehood is a trap! Males, let's get out of this trap together—all the real men, please stand up!!

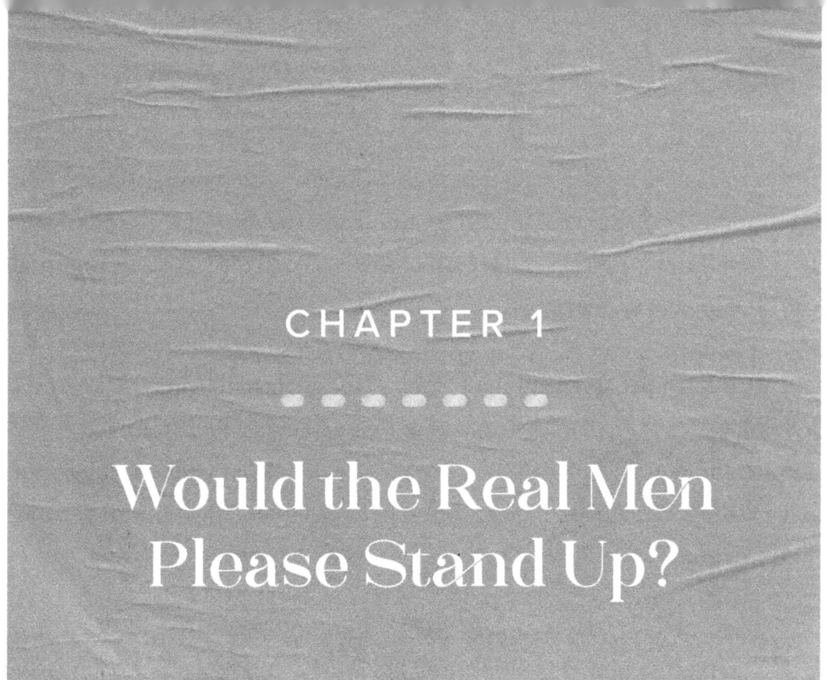

CHAPTER 1

Would the Real Men Please Stand Up?

In order to live as we were designed to live, we must be in pursuit not simply of manhood but of godly masculinity.
— Bob Lepine, *The Christian Husband*

All men are male, but *not* all males are men. Which category are you in? God created men to lead. So, as a man, you must assume the position of captain of the ship called family. It is men's responsibility to steer our families with purpose and integrity. Those who refuse to take command are abandoning their duty. We don't need deserters—we need true captains! As a man, your role is to guide your family in every way. You are at the helm, but if you don't take on your role, someone else will.

CREATED TO LEAD

Genesis 1:26 says "And God said, Let us make man in our image, after our likeness: and let them have dominion over the fish of the sea, and over the fowl of the air, and over the cattle, and over all the earth, and over every creeping thing that creepeth upon the earth" (KJV). On day six, God made man and set the stage for man to oversee everything. Genesis 2:7 continues, "And the LORD God formed man of the dust of the ground, and breathed into his nostrils the breath of life; and man became a **living soul**" (KJV, emphasis added).

This scripture separates man from all other created beings. Mankind is a living soul. All men and women are living beings who can imagine, create, dream, emote, pursue passions, and set their own wills. Animals cannot perform these higher functions. Therefore, the animalkind is separate from mankind.

We belong to our own kingdom, mankind. We belong to our own race, the human race. There is only one race, so all other creatures outside of mankind are of the animal race. Since animals do not have a soul, the soul of a man places him at the top in the hierarchy of all natural living beings. If anyone disagrees with this arrangement, then you should question God because He set it up the way He wanted it, based on His purpose for us.

LEAD WITH PURPOSE

We all have purpose. Our purpose is evident in the fact that we are here. Every individual on earth is unique, and each one brings something of value that can contribute to this world. No two people are alike. History teaches us how people have accepted the challenge of life to fulfill their godly mission while on this earth. What was Martin Luther King's purpose? What was Einstein's purpose? What was Steve Jobs's purpose? These men served in the capacity in which they were created to serve. And our purpose is trapped inside of us, just waiting to be discovered.

Only those who search deep can find their purpose. This purpose is kingdom-minded and has eternal consequences. This is actually our *real* purpose—what God intended for us to accomplish for Him. Mine is different from yours, and yours is different from mine, but both are a reality.

Our souls have infinite value. God compares the worth of one soul to that of the entire world: "For what shall it profit a man, if he shall gain the whole world, and lose his own soul?" (Mark 8:36, KJV).

In God's view, one soul is immensely more valuable than all the gold, platinum, land, real estate, money, and resources contained in the whole world. If every man could fully acknowledge the meaning of Mark 8:36, he would realize that his time is short, his resources are unlimited, and his divine purpose must be pursued with passion. He would realize that he was created to lead because he is valuable.

MEASURING A MAN'S VALUE

Your soul is composed of your mind (your thoughts and ideas), your emotions (how you feel about things), and your will (what you set out to do). Your soul is who you really are. If we subtract all your organs, your weight, your hair, your nails, and all the rest of your physical self, and there is no part of you left to touch, we finally get down to the real you. Would the real you please stand up? Real men stand up because they want to be accounted for. Real men want this world to know they were here.

For some men, it's possible to sum up all of their life accomplishments with the dash on their tombstones between their dates of birth and death. Does that describe you? I hope not. Personally, I refuse to be characterized by a dash on a headstone. My life will be meaningful. You will not look for my headstone at all because the evidence that I have been here will be obvious.

Every person who doubts their meaning or identity should look in the mirror right now and say, "My life has purpose." Say it three times every morning. Your life has meaning. God did not make a mistake in creating you! If people call you illegitimate, then tell them, "My parents may have been illegitimate, but I had no say in the matter." Tell them, "I am one of millions of sperm cells that made it. I am somebody." There are no illegitimate children, only illegitimate parents!

Orison Swett Marden wrote, "There can be no failure to a man who has not lost his courage, his character, his self-respect, or his self-confidence. He is still a king."[4] As a man, it is up to you to filter all the conversations that come from the outside, but—more importantly—to filter the conversations that are happening in your mind right now. Some conversations are optimistic, others can be self-destructive, others can be deeply negative or even suicidal. Every man I know has the same thought processes, but some men are better at filtering these conversations and getting to the truth. Some are better at selecting good thoughts that lead to happiness and joy, but others choose negative thoughts that lead to pain and suffering.

Philippians 4:8 puts it this way: "Finally, brethren, whatsoever things are true, whatsoever things are honest, whatsoever things are just, whatsoever things are pure, whatsoever things are lovely, whatsoever things are of good report; if there be any virtue, and if there be any praise, think on these things" (KJV). To be a man, it is an absolute must that you build your own filter based on who you are according to God's Word. All of our thoughts need sifting from time to time so that we can reach the place where we know who we are in God and we know who God is in us.

You are a living soul, and your value is infinite. The value of a man is built into his infrastructure—the fact that you are here tells me that you have value. And if you attach your value to God, it will never end. Weak men attach their value to things like athletic prowess, womanizing, or

---

4 Orison Swett Marden, *The Optimistic Life* (Thomas Y. Crowell & Co., 1907), 212.

materialism. Sadly, these are temporal and have an expiration date. Attach your value to your heavenly Father. God has no expiration date. He is infinite, which makes your value infinite!

KNOW YOUR ROLE

Some people think God is a male chauvinist because He put men in charge, but the truth is He created men and women equal in value and worth. However, we have different roles in the world, especially in the family unit.

Men were created leaders, so love, integrity, reason, and emotional fortitude should be standard equipment for all men. Men and women have different responsibilities in this earthly realm. Women bring love, nurturing, emotional understanding, and affection to a family. Men, however, provide direction, confidence, and identity.

To lead an entire family, a man must sharpen his Godlike qualities so that he will be successful before God and before his family. You are your family's representative to God in all matters, so choose wisdom over ignorance, choose strength over weakness, choose direction over indecisiveness, choose reason over doubt, and choose faith over fear!

Modern men are not accountable to their families. However, men in previous generations performed better because they accepted the challenges that come with the job. Historically, men made it seem effortless while fighting wars, raising families, working, and paying bills. They refused to skip their responsibilities.

NOT ALL MALES ARE MEN

Men are created leaders, and we have God-given value that is standard for all males. I am frankly disappointed that most of us have been misinformed about our roles as men. But we can set the bar for what it takes to step into manhood.

It is possible to teach every young male to be a man. It is possible to teach them that they can grow, mature, and graduate into what God intends for them to be. Let them know that they can fill that void in their families, churches, and communities. Show them the excitement associated with fulfilling the role they were created to fulfill.

I encourage every male to pray and seek God for wisdom on what it really takes to be a man. Scripture suggests in James 1:5 that "If any of you lacks wisdom, let him ask of God, that giveth to all men liberally, and upbraideth not; and it shall be given him" (KJV).

There are few, if any, rites of passage to manhood anymore. Rites of passage are ceremonial events used to mark the milestone of leaving boyhood and entering manhood. In an independent-thinking world, where every man is for himself, we have no community-based rules to signify maturity. Does age 18 make you a man? Yes, by law, but I am sure you know many 18-year-olds who act like 12-year-olds. Marriage was somewhat of a rite of passage in the past, and maybe getting a "real" job was one too, since it signified the ability to take care of oneself and one's family. But the rites of passage into manhood are just not clear enough for boys trying to become men in the modern era.

This entire book is about helping boys become men, so let's ask God to open our eyes to the full meaning of manhood. Commit to caring for your family—your sons, daughters, and every child you are in authority over. Commit to not entering fatherhood until you are married. Use your position to lead, love, empower, and equip.

It takes a real man to be a true leader. All men are male, but not all males are men. Can we accurately call you male or man? Would your parents call you male or man? Would your spouse call you male or man? My definition of man is as follows: he is a living soul with infinite value, created by God to lead and to love God, himself, his family, and his neighbor. If we can define manhood biblically, then we can appreciate the skills it takes to step into manhood.

If you are male, you have all the necessary tools to be a real man. No one can deny this fact. So, everything about you must align with whom God created you to be.

So recognize that men are created from birth to be leaders, and their value was given to them by God. This value is standard for all males. Pray and ask God to help you understand what it really means to be a man. Ask God to open your eyes to all the facets of maleness and manhood. Commit to correcting every subpar area of your life, and commit to taking care of your family. Commit to helping the grown boys in your community become men.

It takes a real man to be a true leader. The skills to be a man are many, but they can be learned, nurtured, and perfected. And that's exactly what we'll talk about next: the skills men need to pay the bills of life.

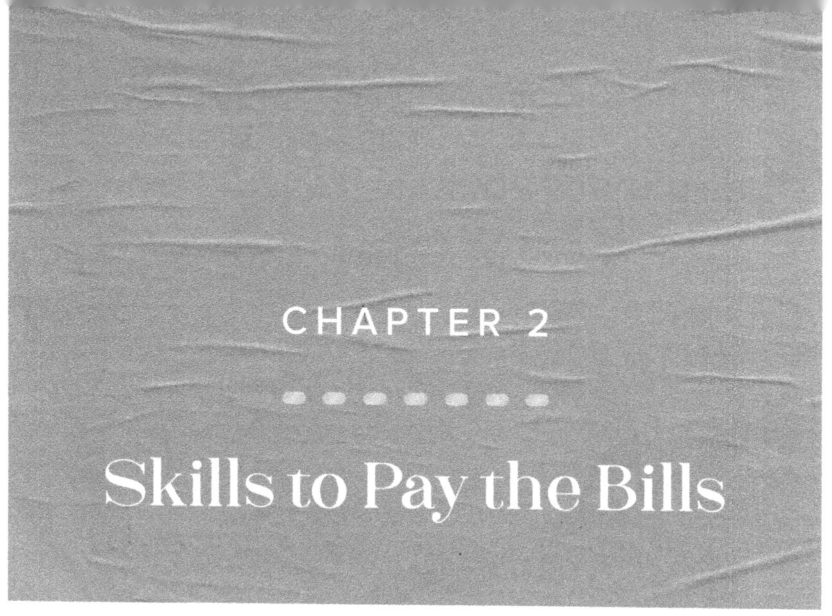

CHAPTER 2

Skills to Pay the Bills

Try not to become a man of success, but rather
try to become a man of value.
— Albert Einstein

ASK EVERY GROWN boy this question: Why should we call you a man when you have "boy" written all over your face? Many of our males' actions speak so loudly that we can't hear what they're saying!

Most adult males invest time in their jobs, their cars, and their hobbies, but how much time do you invest in being a man? Time invested in being a strong man and father will be time well spent, and this investment will pay you for the rest of your life. Actions talk, so males who scream "I am a man" will never convince me that they really are men until they show us what they've got. The skills to reach manhood come from God. These skills are learnable, and it's possible for every male to master them. In this chapter, I will teach you how.

AN UNEXPECTED MAN CARD REQUIREMENT: *LOVE*

To be a real man, you first have to love God and love yourself. It is impossible to love others if you do not love yourself. Traumatic experiences such as father abandonment, mother abandonment, and sexual, emotional, or physical trauma can create a wedge between your heart and that thing called love. This trauma can lead to displaced emotions where you are mad at the world. Let's discuss one example, demonstrated by a prominent figure who is considered one of the best rappers of all time, Tupac Shakur.

Tupac Shakur, an African American rapper who grew up with no father and a crack-addicted mother, had a song called "Me Against the World."

This song has 10 references to death, dying, and killing and three references to shooting alone. It is a snapshot into the mindset and pain of fatherless kids.

Now imagine all the fatherless kids in *your* community with the same mentality as Tupac Shakur. The song makes references to being unloved—imagine what it feels like to have an unloved existence. I have no idea what an unloved life is like. Being unloved is heartbreaking—and think of the kids in your church or at your school who live unloved.

My parents were married when I was born, and they were still together when my dad died in 2014, so I do not know what it means to be abandoned, rejected, or unloved by the people who are supposed to love you. My heart goes out to Mr. Shakur because you can almost feel his pain in the song, but his feelings in the song are foreign to me. However, I am willing to guess that there are countless young men and women in your community who feel exactly like he did.

According to author June Hunt, "Repeated rejection is the breeding ground for low self-worth."[5] It is easy to make the leap from fatherlessness to emotional illness (anger/depression/bitterness) and then to crime, murder, and suicide when rejection is your daily mental diet.

For some reason, many people think guns kill people. That's wrong thinking. Guns do not kill people—broken and rejected people kill people. Guns are amoral, just like bricks, wood, or money. They can be used to shoot deer for a tenderloin dinner, or they can be used to kill people. Similarly, bricks and money can be used to build schools or strip clubs. I have been fascinated with guns all my life, but I do not plan to shoot anyone.

What was the fate of Mr. Tupac Shakur? Did he shoot someone? He rapped about sex, violence, and immorality in almost all his songs, and before he could kill someone, he was gunned down in Las Vegas on September 7, 1996. Was the culprit the gun, or was it the shooter? The answer to this question is obvious, so let's stay focused on the problem—rejected, abandoned fatherless boys who have no direction and no respect for human life because no one respected their lives.

An unloved child has a hard time loving anyone—including himself. An unloved child develops anger issues, resentment, bitterness, and hatred. This hatred stems from unreciprocated love from an absentee father. But since the father is playing "ghost," these emotions are acted out on whomever is closest or whomever gets in the way.

How does trauma affect the heart of a child? In my five decades of life, I have noticed how trauma becomes a roadblock to normal emotional and spiritual child development, especially in boys. Trauma in the form of fatherlessness seems to arrest an individual's emotional growth. This arrested

5 June Hunt, *Self-Worth: Discover Your God-Given Worth* (AspirePress, 2013), 9.

development is why father rejection is the worst trauma of all! It is the underlying catalyst for an unloved society.

When fathers are absent from families, it leads to poverty, crime, teen pregnancy, high school dropouts, and homelessness. Absent fathers guarantee the lucrative profits of private prison owners. Their absence also guarantees long careers for judges, district attorneys, criminal defense attorneys, detectives, probation officers, and police officers.

Fatherlessness creates a divided heart and spirit, and those divisions usually bear out in the ultimate destiny of the fatherless child. Children with divided minds have unclear direction and difficulty finding their places in society. Fear, rather than courage, drives them.

Trauma can be uninvited and oftentimes criminal, but when a child has an absentee father, they often interpret this as "my father hates me." These ghost dads are like phantoms to their kids, who feel that they are out there somewhere, but they cannot touch them. Children of ghost dads feel unloved.

Loving someone means being involved and present. But these faulty fathers do not know how to love because they do not know the God of love. Jesus explains love like this in Matthew 22:36–40: "Master, which is the great commandment in the law? Jesus said unto him, Thou shalt love the Lord thy God with all thy heart, and with all thy soul, and with all thy mind. This is the first and great commandment. And the second is like unto it, Thou shalt love thy neighbor as thyself. On these two commandments hang all the law and the prophets" (KJV).

Jesus was answering a Pharisee (a religious teacher of the day), and He basically gave the prescription for pleasing God. You must love God first, then love yourself, which then gives you the emotional capacity to love everyone else. The simple version of this is love your neighbor like you love yourself.

A male who hates himself has great difficulty loving others. He has difficulty loving his kids, and he thinks nothing of walking up to another person and shooting their brains out. It's not guns, but rather lack of love that has incited the violence and crime we see in America today. Lack of respect for the sanctity of life leads to crime. Remember, guns do not kill people—broken people kill people.

The trauma of father abandonment leads to self-hatred and low self-worth, and this process is the catalyst for disenfranchisement, disillusionment, and complete disconnect from human values. We are God's most intellectual creatures, but we fail at the most basic principles of survival: take care of and protect your own.

Fatherless young men seek father figures from whom acceptance is the norm, whether those "father figures" come in the forms of gangs, high school sports teams, rap groups, or similar. Unloved children just want to be loved. Without fathers, there is no inner sense of identity, so the local gangsters or the high school coach or the most popular rapper of the day becomes the de facto father figure.

Some boys have no father figures at all, so all their decisions are made from ignorance and selfishness. They can't relate to a father's love since they have never experienced a father's love. The Bible puts it this way: "Whoever does not love does not know God, because God is love" (1 John 4:8, NIV). Since He is the ultimate Father, a lack of God in a man's heart leads to a selfish, prideful existence.

Love is the prerequisite to being a man. It takes love to commit to a woman for life, without knowing any details of how this adventure will bear out. It takes love to care for children in every way imaginable. It takes love to tirelessly sacrifice without recognition from anyone. It takes love to care enough for yourself to go to annual doctor visits, dental visits, and other preventive care visits. You surely must love yourself to get a prostate exam; it will *not* be a pleasant experience. But it must be done to prevent one of the most curable forms of cancer, prostate cancer.

A father's love is the most critical element to developing a child. A mother's love is critical especially in the younger years, but frankly, every study on parenting proves *both* parents are necessary to raise healthy children. Torri J. Evans-Barton, founder of the Fatherless Generation Foundation, says, "When fathers are actively present in the lives of their children, it validates their children's very existence."[6] Without a father's love, it is hard for a boy to reciprocate something he has never received or understood. Boys and girls have tried for ages to grow up without dads, but the verdict is in on what fatherlessness can do:

— 85% of youth who are currently in prison grew up in a fatherless home.
— 7 out of every 10 youth that are housed in state-operated correctional facilities, including detention and residential treatment, come from a fatherless home.
— Children from fatherless homes are twice as likely to drop out from school before graduating than children who have a father in their lives.
— Girls who live in a fatherless home have a 100% higher risk of suffering from obesity than girls who have their father present. Teen girls from fatherless homes are also 4 times more likely to become mothers before the age of 20.
— In [2021], [35%] of children in homes headed by a single mother were living in poverty.[7]

---

6 Cedric Wright, "The Solution to the Fatherless Pandemic," 24-7 Press Release, October 27, 2022, https://www.24-7pressrelease.com/press-release/495426/the-solution-to-the-fatherless-pandemic.

7 "Poverty Status of Children by Family Structure," Office of Juvenile Justice and Delinquency Prevention, accessed September 17, 2025, https://ojjdp.ojp.gov/statistical-briefing-book/population/faqs/qa01203.

— Children who live in a single-parent home are more than 2 times more likely to commit suicide than children in a two-parent home.
— 72% of Americans believe that a fatherless home is the most significant social problem and family problem that is facing their country.
— 75% of rapists are motivated by displaced anger that is associated with feelings of abandonment that involves their father.
— Living in a fatherless home is a contributing factor to substance abuse, with children from such homes accounting for 75% of adolescent patients being treated in substance abuse centers.
— 85% of all children which exhibit some type of a behavioral disorder come from a fatherless home.
— 90% of the youth in the United States who decide to run away from home, or become homeless for any reason, originally come from a fatherless home.
— 63% of youth suicides involve a child who was living in a fatherless home when they made their final decision.[8]

In addition, fatherlessness is the single greatest predictor of suicide among young men.[9]

Fatherless children suffer from a lack of identity, a lack of direction, and most of all, a lack of love. Fatherless children know something is missing. Some discover the missing link and recruit father figures in their communities and churches. Some never discover why they struggle in all areas of life. In case you are wondering, direction, identity, confidence, and love are the main principles fathers bring to the family.

8 "Thirty-Six Shocking Statistics on Fatherless Homes," Life Is Beautiful Ministries of Faith, October 4, 2018, https://lifeisbeautiful.org/statistics-on-fatherless-homes.

9 Warren Farrell and John Grey, *The Boy Crisis: Why Our Boys Are Struggling and What We Can Do About It* (BenBella Books, 2018).

There is some confusion in our world about the importance of fathers, but these statistics are a painful reminder that fathers are absolutely necessary to the creation of a better society.

God's plan for the family has worked for thousands of years. This precedent was set by our Creator, and it is the best model known to mankind. Men are the primary leaders and hold the greater weight of responsibility for the outcomes of their families. Weak men make weak families. Loveless men make loveless families. Irresponsible men make irresponsible families. Love is the ultimate bond that makes real men sacrifice everything for their families.

Working and paying bills is only half of your responsibility as a man. The other half includes providing spiritual leadership, offering discipline, giving direction, helping your kids identify their gifts, spending time with them, and listening to them. This list is infinitely long, but real men do these things with intentionality and with all seriousness.

Leading a family is securing the next generation. Leading a family is securing *your* golden years, Dad. You are the leader, and if the ship sinks, it is your fault! The reason the current generation suffers so much is due to their fatherless existence.

A friend of mine who is over 40 years old still pines for his father, even though his parents have been divorced for over 20 years. He pulls up old texts from his dad that were sent to him over 10 years ago. He tries to reach out to his dad on social media, but his dad is not interested. This young man has had drug problems and multiple divorces, and he cannot place his feet solidly on the grounds of life. Family splits are like nuclear bombs going off, and the aftermath can be devastating for kids.

A CULTURE OF GROWN BOYS

Modern times have produced a culture of grown boys who refuse to acknowledge that they are children trapped in men's bodies. It becomes easy for a grown boy to leave his family and kids when times are tough because he has no understanding of fatherly love. Remember, he thinks like a boy, so he is unsure of what responsibility looks like. But love makes a real man refuse to leave.

The wife of a friend of mine was addicted to drugs. Ultimately, my friend had to sell his vehicles, business, home, and land to generate the funds for her rehabilitation. He lost everything and had to change careers just to get out of debt, but he never left his wife. I have the utmost respect for my friend because he loves his wife and kids more than his wife loves drugs. His passion for his family conquered her passion for drugs! Passion conquers passion.

Love comes from God since God is love: "He that loveth not, knoweth not God; for God is love" (1 John 4:8, KJV). No man can truthfully say he loves his kids if he forfeits responsibility and passes the buck to someone else.

If God is love, then what does it look like to love practically? The Bible tells us, "Love is patient and kind; love does not envy or boast; it is not arrogant or rude. It does not insist on its own way; it is not irritable or resentful; it does not rejoice at wrongdoing, but rejoices with the truth. Love bears all things, believes all things, hopes all things, endures all things" (1 Corinthians 13:4–8, ESV).

Love is patient. Love is not arrogant. Love does not insist on its own way. Love is not selfish or self-serving. Love does not run at the first sign of trouble. Love is the most important factor in becoming a man and in becoming a great husband and father. But without love, a child can easily descend into a life of crime and perpetually search for what's missing in all the wrong places. On the other hand, true love builds not only people, but entire cultures. With love, forgiveness and growth take place in the minds of males seeking manhood. Without love, bitterness and self-hate invade the minds of our young men.

Explain to all males that hugs are standard material for men. Children deserve lots of love, so fathers should say "I love you" regularly. Fathers should coach their sons in T-ball, flag football, basketball, and any other engagement that maximizes their time spent together. Spending time together is how you tell your kids you love them.

Children should worship ***with*** their parents on Sundays. The model you set as a man and parent determines what your kids believe about life. Fathers should eat dinners with their families, pray with their families, and teach their families the ways of God.

Homes should be safe places where love is everywhere. Fathers should get their cues from God and the Bible. The older generation must teach the next generation of males how to love, lead, and live productive lives. The goal is not perfect children, but completeness in God. Our goal is not to be perfect men, but successful men.

As a child, I was ridiculed. I was called a nerd. However, when I went home, my parents would tell me I could be anything I wanted to be in life. They told me I was somebody. They constantly reinforced that thought process, and today I still believe it! I cannot remember one specific conversation with my parents about being something in life, but the underlying theme was that I could do anything I set my mind to. The underlying theme to my life is that no one is better than me.

Remember the quote from earlier: "There can be no failure to a man who has not lost his courage, his character, his self-respect, or his self-confidence. He is still a king."[10] I have lived by this quote all through college, medical school, and my career. Where did my secure way of thinking come from? My dad gave me the confidence to believe that dreams are possible, and my mom nurtured the thoughts long enough for me to never forget them. Oh, the power of loving parents!

Love can keep any marriage together, and love will saturate your kids' hearts to continue the cycle. Love builds confidence. Love is a token of God that makes the heart hope for better. Love is an action, not a feeling. Feelings change like the wind, so they are unreliable. But an act of love lasts through eternity. Scripture says in 1 Peter 4:8 that "love covers a multitude of sins" (ESV). Love is powerful.

So, let's invest time in the skills to pay the bills of manhood and fatherhood. Since these skills are learnable, every male should be courageous enough to discover what's missing in his own life, fix it, and move forward. No man is perfect, and no father is perfect, so eliminate that train of thought.

A good place to start learning is Genesis in the Bible. Another good source is *Understanding the Purpose and Power of Men* by Myles Munroe. Surround yourself with strong men who have been through the fires of life but stand strong despite what they have been through. To be called man takes emotional strength and personal investment that starts within. Our battle to manhood is not external—it is internal.

In a world lacking the inner strength needed in men, we create a huge storm of pleasure-seeking, emotion-driven, superficial men who lack accountability.

---

10 Marden, *The Optimistic Life*, 212.

THE NEW IQ MEN NEED

My greatest challenge in life is emotional intelligence (also known as emotional IQ), particularly translating my feelings into words. Men are strong, but sometimes our strength can be our undoing. One of my business partners is exceptionally intelligent, and he has a lucrative career. By all accounts, he is smart and accomplished, and he should have the emotional intelligence to match his other personal skills.

He married a phone saleswoman who was lazy and had no goals—and, oh, she had a drug problem too. After two kids and multiple drug rehab stints, he divorced her. He and I would talk, and he would always go back to "What was I thinking by marrying her?" In other words, why hadn't he, the smart rich guy, understood this woman emotionally on a deeper level *before* he married her? He admitted that he had lacked emotional understanding, and it had cost him his marriage.

Reading another person's emotions—and reading your own—is a skill that generally comes easily to women. They master it effortlessly. But men tend to be more emotionally structured and rigid. In addition, we simply lack empathy at times, making us unable to fully appreciate the emotions of others. This deficit of emotion is a weakness for most men. It will require honest effort and work to gain mastery of this skill.

I have no daughters, so I have mainly had to understand my wife's and sons' thoughts, feelings, and emotions. We all have an internal thermometer that allows us to determine the emotional temperature of those around us, but most men's thermometers are broken. How do we read another person's emotions? By getting to know them!

Spending time with our kids is the primary activity that will afford us a higher grade on the emotional IQ scale. Kids spell "love" like this: *T-I-M-E.* Patience, especially when our kids are in their developmental years, is an absolute must. Otherwise, your hair will gray prematurely. There is no one way to learn everything about the members of our families, but learning as much as we can is the goal. Every child is different, so we might not be able to understand one child as well as we do another. Nevertheless, reading your child's heart will make you one of the best dads in the world. Schedule activities that allow you and your child to connect. Spend time in different venues that allow teachable moments, and always have a teacher's heart.

Emotions can be fickle and may mislead us at times, so we should never make decisions based on emotions alone. Young men in particular could avoid many pitfalls in life if they followed this advice. I am certain many young Black men would still be alive if they knew how to control their emotions.

Being stopped by a police officer is not an activity that requires anger. The police officer is just doing his job. Most Black men I know, including me, have been stopped for "DWB"—driving while Black—but this is no occasion for bravado. Why would you provoke a man who has a baton, handcuffs, mace, a taser, a bulletproof vest, and a gun? If you provoke a man like that, there is one word for you: *dumb!*

My dad taught me to respect the position the police officer is in, even if I don't respect the man. The position places him in authority over me during our interaction, but I will live to tell the story. I will not escalate the situation further. For all I know, the officer could be headed to divorce court, about to lose his family. For all I know, he could be in bankruptcy, or he could have a child who just overdosed on drugs. Police officers are real people with real problems—like everyone else. Yes, professionalism is required of them, but good citizenship is required for young men.

I remember a time when I was stopped by a police officer while in college. I was driving from the University of Southern Mississippi (USM) campus one night in a Ford Escort on Highway 49 North in Hattiesburg, Mississippi. A Caucasian police officer pulled me over and said I had blasted through a red light. (The light was yellow.) It was just after midnight, and the police officer asked me where I was going. I told him I was going back to my sister's house. After looking at my driver's license, he asked for my USM ID. (I didn't know you had to have a college ID to drive.)

The police officer asked me to step out of the car and stand in front of his cruiser with my hands on the hood. I promptly did exactly as he said. He opened the trunk and thoroughly searched my car, my book bag, my spare tire well, and my glove compartment. He then asked me if I had anything in the car that I was not supposed to have. I replied, "Yes, my dad's gun is under the driver's seat." I was still standing with my hands on his cruiser with my legs spread. He retrieved the gun, unloaded it, then walked back to the cruiser. During this entire 30-minute encounter at midnight on the side of the road, my emotions never changed. My feelings at this time were "If he thinks I am doing something wrong, then he has a right to do what he is doing. If he thinks I am breaking the law, then he can arrest me; I certainly won't try to stop him."

He walked back over to me in front of the cruiser and said, "Mr. Hall, you could get in trouble with that unregistered gun in there." "Give your dad his gun back, and have a good night." No citation was given.

Most of you might have thought I would have been the victim of police violence, but my father taught me to respect myself first. If a man respects himself, he has no problem respecting others.

I did not run that red light. I was tired, sleepy, and ready to get home, but I complied with the officer's line of questioning, answering "yes, sir" where necessary. Always have command of your emotions—even if a police officer unfairly pulls you over. In case you forgot, that is what they were hired to do—to pull people over. And if you are an American citizen, you pay them to do that. If you don't want to be pulled over, stay home. If you are too emotionally unstable to interact with an officer of the law, stay home. I have never cursed a police officer out, and I never will. I am apologetic to police officers and super nice to them. Most of my traffic stops end just like the one above. I have *never* been arrested, threatened, slammed down, or roughhoused by a police officer, and I am a Black man living in Mississippi.

If you give respect, you will get respect. Real men handle their emotions well. Two-year-old toddlers throw temper tantrums because they don't get their way. Grown boys curse, yell, and attempt to hide evidence when it comes time to face the consequences of their actions. And when they react in this way, it usually does not end well. Most police officers want to drink coffee, eat doughnuts, get paid for it, and go home. Laugh out loud, because I believe this is true. Police officers do not want to shoot young men on the side of the road and then spend two hours typing up reports.

Nothing is certain, but if you have a good command of your emotions, that ensures good decision-making, sound judgment, and logical thinking. These are characteristics of men.

Men lead with logic and reason. Women think with their emotions, but men think with logic. That does not mean women are less than men, but it does mean that men make decisions at a different level than women. Different—not better. God made us like this because He wanted balance. Boys raised by women are more emotional, and that lack of emotional control becomes a liability when those boys become men. If one of those boys' girlfriends breaks up with them, he lacks the psychological fortitude it takes to understand that a breakup is a temporary situation. Many breakups have led to murder, suicide, or both at the hands of insecure young men.

For example, B. J. Brown shot his ex-girlfriend, Cassandra Jones, a mother of three, in cold blood on June 27, 2022, over a breakup.[11] Two days later, it happened again. "A 22-year-old man was arrested in connection with the death of Azsia Johnson, a 20-year-old mother who was fatally shot at point blank range on Wednesday as she pushed her 3-month-old daughter in a stroller while on a walk."[12] His name was Isaac Argro, and it happened due to a breakup.[13] Life is hard, and relationships are even harder at times. So, if your emotional bank is empty, there is nothing to withdraw from in difficult times.

Rational decisions evade the minds of angry, broken, testosterone-enriched young men. Just like the delinquent elephants we talked about in the introduction, overly emotional men wreak havoc in their families and communities because men typically act out their emotions. Women, on the other hand, *talk* out their emotions.

When a boy has always been told yes by his mother, grandmother, and aunts, he assumes all women are yes-women. However, relationships are the perfect scenarios for conflict to occur. Eventually, the boy finds out that all women are not his mother, and the real world teaches him that hearing no is a regular part of life. Hearing no makes you creative; it makes you think differently; it makes you pray harder; it humbles you; it opens you up to all the other possibilities available.

My dad told me no so many times that once I entered the real world, a no was just a formality to me. A no was kind of funny. It had lost its value

---

11 Keith Phillips, "Murder/Update: Man Who Killed Vicksburg Woman Dies in Prison," *Vicksburg Daily News*, March 2, 2025, https://vicksburgnews.com/murder-update-man-who-killed-vicksburg-woman-dies-in-prison.

12 Chelsia Rose Marcius et al., "Police Eye Domestic Violence in Upper East Side Killing of Mother," *New York Times*, June 30, 2022, https://www.nytimes.com/2022/07/01/nyregion/mother-shot-upper-east-side-father-arrested.html.

13 Jack Morphet et al., "Azsia Johnson's Accused Killer Isaac Argro Was an 'Angry Bird' with Rage Issues, Victim's Mom Says," *New York Post*, last updated July 3, 2022, https://nypost.com/2022/07/02/azsia-johnsons-ex-boyfriend-and-accused-killer-an-angry-bird/.

in my mind because I knew life would go on. It was not even a rejection to me because if I worked hard enough, planned better, and executed better, I knew I could eventually get to a 'yes'.

Mothers simply do not have the full capacity to administer the type of discipline and direction that fathers can. Fathers challenge, but mothers nurture. Both are necessary, so there's obviously something lacking when there is no one to deposit one of these values into a child.

A person can never give what they don't have. Men have the innate capacity to set standards so that boundaries are created in their children's hearts. Undisciplined children are usually emotionally bankrupt. This deficit is why there is an epidemic of grown boys.

AVOID THE IDENTITY CRISIS

Character starts in the womb. Just knowing that there are two people who care about you builds character. Having a father, not just a sperm donor, gives a child a sense of identity, which is the foundation of self-worth and purpose. Identity is the breeding ground for purpose!

How silly is it for us to expect a fatherless child to have exceptional purpose and self-awareness, when he has no male connection to the world? In that case, there is no attachment, and there are no identifying markers of where the child comes from. This unattached life creates a void in the child's soul.

Roland Warren, the former president of the National Fatherhood Initiative, says, "Every child has a hole in his or her heart in the shape of their dad."[14] There is a void in the mind, emotions, and will of fatherless

---

14 Roland Warren, "When Men and Fathers Commit to Help a Fatherless Boy," National Fatherhood Initiative, last updated January 3, 2018, https://www.fatherhood.org/championing-fatherhood/when-men-and-fathers-commit-to-help-a-fatherless-boy.

children. And as we know, nature abhors a vacuum! Unfilled space will be filled with something. To all you absentee fathers, what is filling your child's heart right now?

Fatherlessness is the primary traumatic event that disconnects a child from character and purpose. Fatherlessness may be the greatest trauma of all because it means "I have been rejected for just being here, though this has nothing to do with my own existence."

Remember, "Repeated rejection is the breeding ground for low self-worth."[15] Rejection compels the heart to forget societal norms. Rejection also decreases a person's innate value so much that most fatherless children have inferiority complexes, insecurity complexes, and fear complexes.

Repeated rejection can make a person do strange things. Remember, rejection is why fatherlessness is the single greatest predictor of suicide among young men.[16] Rejection is why "90% of the youth in the United States who decide to run away from home, or become homeless for any reason, originally come from a fatherless home."[17] Rejection is why "75% of rapists are motivated by displaced anger that is associated with feelings of abandonment that involves their father."[18] According to the *Daily Mail*, "Growing up without a father could permanently alter the structure of the brain and produce children who are more aggressive and angry, scientists have warned."[19]

Character starts at the level of the parents, so if only one parent is present, the hole in a child's character may grow exponentially. It doesn't

15 Hunt, *Self-Worth*, 9.
16 Farrell and Grey, *Boy Crisis*.
17 "Thirty-Six Shocking Statistics."
18 "Thirty-Six Shocking Statistics."
19 Ben Spector, "Growing Up Without a Father Can Permanently Alter the Brain: Fatherless Children Are More Likely to Grow Up Angry and Then Turn to Drugs," December 4, 2013, *Daily Mail*, https://www.dailymail.co.uk/sciencetech/article-2518247/Growing-father-permanently-alter-BRAIN-Fatherless-children-likely-grow-angry-turn-drugs.html.

surprise me to see a fatherless boy walk up to a person and shoot that person's brains out for no reason. Lack of character and lack of identity makes people do this.

When a child has no father, that means that they will have a certain degree of lack of identity and character. Kids with no identity live without acknowledged intrinsic value. There is no meaningful value trapped inside of their minds because the identity factor, their dad, is missing. Boys with earrings, tattoos, and sagging pants to their knees have no real identity, so they identify with the culture instead of identifying with family.

As a matter of fact, any person with an identity crisis searches for imitations to fill what's missing. These imitations may come in the form of body markings, drugs, violence, promiscuity, or complete apathy. Children who know their identities usually identify with their parents and with the god of their parents. There is value in knowing your identity. There is eternal value in knowing who you are and why you are on Earth. Fathers bring these factors to the family. Lacking identity means lacking purpose, which means lacking character. Character deficits are created by father abandonment!

Some communities think that the "strong woman," or matriarch of the family, is what's necessary to build character-enriched communities. If you believe this, please go back to chapter 2 and read those fatherlessness stats again. This book would have no value if these fatherlessness statistics were not real. There is a gross miscalculation at play in the modern era that says men are disposable. It says that men are not valuable to the success of the family. On the contrary—men are critically important to family and child development!

A friend recently shared that her daughters both experienced major psychological problems when she divorced. One daughter was diagnosed with bipolar disorder, and the other daughter became angry and rebellious.

Both daughters stayed with their mom after the split. There is a fundamental temperament crystallized in the hearts of a child when Dad is present. No one can refute this. No one. The statistics support this statement, history supports it, the Bible supports it, God supports it, and every child living with his father supports it!

I hear people bring up exceptions to these stats, but honestly, we do not live based on exceptions. We live based on truth. We live based on what is right and what is wrong. We live based on what is best for our children, and having a father and mother in the home is the best scenario for a child. If you disagree with this, please *do not* have any children.

According to the CDC, the percent of births occurring to unmarried Black women is 69%.[20] The Institute for Family Studies published an analysis in its report *Stronger Families, Safer Streets* that indicated that the total crime rate in cities with high levels of single parenthood was 48% higher than that in those with low levels of single parenthood. When it comes to violent crime and homicide, cities with high levels of single parenthood have 188% higher rates of violence and 255% higher rates of homicide.[21] These are not coincidences. This is the result of real people being held back by their moms and dads.

No one can stop a person from accomplishing their dreams. However, if we eliminate fatherhood from any culture, that culture will suffer. This reasoning is not rocket science. Sadly, though, it is easier to play the blame game instead of finding the root of the problem. Black people are the only ones who can resolve the crime, poverty, identity crises, and disillusionment in their communities because responsibility to family is an individual challenge.

---

20 Joyce A. Martin et al., "Births: Final Data for 2018," *National Vital Statistics Reports* 68, no. 13 (2019), https://www.cdc.gov/nchs/data/nvsr/nvsr68/nvsr68_13-508.pdf.

21 Rafael A. Mangual et al., "New Report: Stronger Families, Safer Streets," Institute for Family Studies, December 12, 2023, https://ifstudies.org/blog/new-report-stronger-families-safer-streets-.

Fathers have a huge role to play in society, and love, emotional intelligence, and character are learnable skills. However, without a culture of fatherhood, we see a firestorm of fatherlessness, and this storm has created the world we live in today.

If you would like to live in a better world, do some honest introspection about your lifestyle and your emotional contributions to your family, and make the necessary changes. Take a hard and honest look at each of the skill areas we discussed in this chapter. Then write down what needs to change and how you plan to change it. Your family and children will appreciate it, and they will reap the benefits of a healthy you.

More importantly, teach the young men in your community to do the same. Help them dream about the men they want to be, and show them the importance of building the real skills of manhood.

The root causes of fatherlessness are subtle, but the effects of this moral failure have created a social hurricane in your school, in your church, and in your community. So, let's learn how to navigate that storm together in chapter 3.

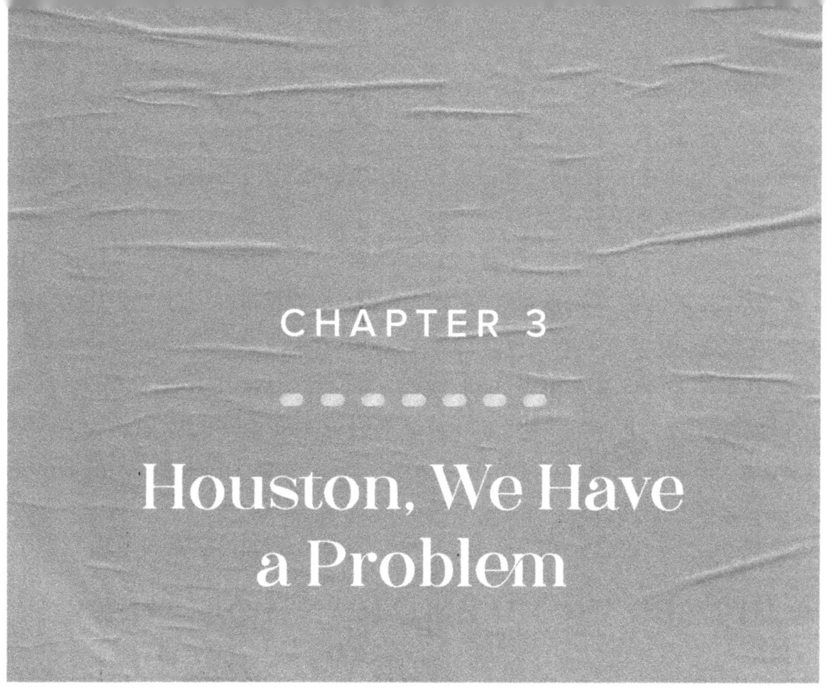

CHAPTER 3

Houston, We Have a Problem

If you don't find the root of the problem, it will continue to grow. You will never happen up on the solution.
— Unknown

FATHERLESSNESS IS THE Hurricane Katrina of the modern family. Absentee fathers and weak men are like the bureaucratic crooks who prevented levee maintenance, ultimately leading to disaster. But the bigger issue is that *no one knew where the weak spots were.*

Maybe you are the flimsy embankment in our society today. Hurricane Katrina hit the American Gulf Coast on August 29, 2005. It was a Category 3 hurricane and was the most devastating storm since the Okeechobee hurricane of 1928. The economic cost of Hurricane Katrina was estimated to be $170 billion, making it the costliest storm in American history.[22] According to Wikipedia, "The largest loss of life during the storm was due to flooding caused by engineering flaws in the

22 Sarah Pruitt, "Hurricane Katrina: Ten Facts About the Deadly Storm and Its Legacy," History.com, accessed July 1, 2025, https://www.history.com/articles/hurricane-katrina-facts-legacy.

federally built hurricane flood protection system, particularly the levees around New Orleans, LA."[23]

Many people felt like state and federal officials neglected their duties in levee maintenance, and this contributed to New Orleans flooding. The crime, poverty, and homelessness we see today prove someone has neglected their duties in the realm of family and morality. The storm we are discussing in this chapter involves dads, moms, and kids, with fathers neglecting their responsibilities to be storm ready.

A BIGGER PROBLEM THAN YOU THINK

The problem is not racism. America makes up 4% of the world's population,[24] and compared to most other countries, I believe we have done more to end racism than the other 96% of the world. America recognized its problem and, at the highest degree, signed, ratified, and enacted legislation specifically designed to end the darkest hour of our history.

Are there lasting effects from slavery, racism, and Jim Crow? Yes. Absolutely. There is such a thing as post-traumatic slavery syndrome, but if we place all the blame on slavery and racism, we will ignore all the other causes of fatherlessness and family dissolution. Some think we are perpetual victims of slavery, discrimination, and prejudice, but victimhood stops when you decide that you will not play that card anymore.

Slavery cannot perpetually victimize you. Nothing is permanent, so only immature people who refuse to grow up stay in victim mode. We are moving in the wrong direction because of choice—not the past. Our past does not have to predict our future, so please stop blaming racism,

---

23 Wikipedia, "Hurricane Katrina," last modified June 16, 2025, 22:25 (UTC), https://en.wikipedia.org/wiki/Hurricane_Katrina.

24 "U.S. and World Population Clock," United States Census Bureau, accessed July 7, 2025, at 23:10 UTC), https://www.census.gov/popclock/.

prejudice, and discrimination for the breakdown of the family unit. The problem is deeper than that.

If we assume only minority communities suffer at the hands of fatherlessness, we have forgotten that fatherlessness affects all communities! The problem is not crime—crime is a result of the problem! The problem is not poverty—poverty is a result of the problem! The problem has several layers that start with the choices we men make.

A PERFECT STORM

A perfect storm has been created in the realm of family, and pretending we don't see it is foolish. This storm has systematically eased fathers out of the home and persuaded them to go derelict in their responsibility to their family. Every problem has a solution, but what's more important than the solution? The underlying series of events that lead to fractured societies. Solutions are reactive, but resolving the root cause of the problem is proactive. In this section, we will discuss the root causes of grown boys in our world and try to fully discover how we ended up here.

PLEASURE-SEEKING MEN

> *This know also, that in the last days perilous times shall come. For men shall be lovers of their own selves, covetous, boasters, proud, blasphemers, disobedient to parents, unthankful, unholy, without natural affection, trucebreakers, false accusers, incontinent, fierce, despisers of those that are good, traitors, heady, high-minded, lovers of pleasures more than lovers of God.*
>
> — 2 Timothy 3:1–4 (KJV)

Men are the targets of every vice known to this world. Alcohol, sex, drugs, and laziness are designed to divert the attention of men and destroy their potential. Men have a bull's-eye on their souls, and our enemy, satan, is very much aware of his target. When men lose the fear of God, they lose reverent respect and awe for God.

"Fear" in this context means to hold in very high regard, so much so that a person's behavior is dictated by that respect and regard. God is not in the business of scaring people. He is in the business of loving and empowering people. He is in the business of blessing people and destroying curses in their lives! Curses like fatherlessness.

Men who have a deep respect for God find it easy to love their wives and children. Men who are selfish find it hard to love anyone. Self-serving and egotistical men constantly look for escape mechanisms—usually in the form of another woman, another hobby, another party, another hit, or another dollar. The list is endless. And this cycle continues with every weak man who refuses to grow up.

Check Your Manhood—or Boyhood

The scripture above says that in the last days men will exhibit the characteristics listed below, which I have divided into 11 categories. I have created a simple self-assessment on manhood using these 11 biblical traits. These traits are classically associated with grown boys, so if you score high on this list, you are part of the problem. You are selfish, pleasure seeking, and lacking in wisdom.

Self-Assessment on Manhood

Go down the list, answering yes if each trait applies to you, no if it does not.

Yes No **Lovers of Their Own Selves:** Narcissistic, self-focused, selfish

Yes No **Covetous:** Greedy, money-loving, materialistic (obsessed with toys like boats, four-wheelers, and guns)

Yes No **Boasters/Proud/Heady/High-Minded:** Arrogant, prideful, conceited, always needing to be right

Yes No **Blasphemers/Unholy:** Profane toward anything godly, irreverent

Yes No **Disobedient to Parents:** Defiant toward parents or authority figures

Yes No **Unthankful:** Ungrateful (for family, job, and possessions), impossible to please

Yes No **Without Natural Affection:** Lacking natural human affection and emotions, callous

Yes No **Trucebreakers/Traitors/False Accusers:** Dishonest, slanderous, deceitful

Yes No **Incontinent:** Lacking self-control (emotionally, financially, sexually, and interpersonally)

Yes No **Fierce/Despisers of Those That Are Good**: Hateful toward anything good, brutal in behavior

Yes No **Lovers of Pleasures More Than Lovers of God**: Pleasure seeking, hedonistic

Use the 11 biblical traits above to check your manhood level.
CHART: Yes or No

< 3 Man (*improvement needed on "yes" items)*
3–5 Immature (*serious improvement needed)*
> 5 Grown Boy (*relationship with God needed*)

If you score fewer than 3 yes answers, you are a man. If you score 3–5 yes answers, you are immature and need a little work. If you score more than 5 yes answers, you are a grown boy.

Man: You are ready to lead, with the understanding that you must surround yourself with men who are more spiritual and godly than you are. A Christian counselor may help you with any emotional baggage you carry from the past. Prayer and Bible reading will help you with deficits in your spirit. If this is you, find a God-filled church and join a men's group so that you can continue to grow.

Immature: You are still acting as if you are 12–18 years old. You are selfish and miserable as a man because you are living a purposeless life. You have not prayed seriously in weeks, if not months. You have not seriously read your Bible for growth and spiritual maturity. You probably go to church, but it is just a box to check to soothe your consciousness. If you are married, you could possibly lose your family any day.

If this describes you, let me challenge you to take the following actions. Seek spiritual and emotional counseling. Pray at least an hour every morning before work, and read your Bible at least 30 minutes every day. Turn your phone off for two hours daily. Forgive anyone who has hurt you from your past (Matthew 6:14–15). Unforgiveness is an entry point for unclean spirits to plant a root of bitterness in your mind. And finally, consider enrolling in our Mighty Men Academy to take your growth into manhood to the next level.

The Mighty Men Academy will help you understand what it means to be a man and will give you practical, real-life ways to lead. Manhood is a learned skill, so this academy focuses on all the raw fundamentals of male leadership and manhood.

Grown Boy: You live only for yourself. Your family is fourth or fifth on your priority list. God is last. Your job is more important than your family. Sports, fishing, and hunting are your idols. You watch a lot of TV, movies, or sports and spend too much time on social media. You can name more pro athletes than men in the Bible.

You could be headed for divorce if you are married. If you are single, do not get married until you resolve these issues! You have a long-distance relationship with God. You should renew your vows with God. Every area of your life needs work. Pride and selfishness will eventually destroy you and your family. As Proverbs 16:18 says, "Pride goeth before destruction, and an haughty spirit before a fall" (KJV).

I suggest you meet with a God-sent pastor on a regular basis to help you grow spiritually, then meet with a Christian counselor on a regular basis to help uncover your emotional deficiencies. What do I mean by "a God-sent pastor"? There are many preachers but only few men of God. Many preachers hold the title of "pastor," but very few have been chosen by God to lead in that capacity.

Grown boys have many character defects. Most people know that you are a grown boy, but they are reluctant to tell you due to your childlike reaction. I am telling you that you never grew up. Being over the age of 18 does not ensure manhood—you have never made the decision to be a man.

If you fit this description, enroll in a church men's group to hold you accountable or get a male accountability partner who will hold you responsible in every area of your life. Enroll in our Mighty Men Academy. Find a good church group with strong leadership, strong men, and programs designed to turn boys into men.

Daddy Issues?

Any male who loves pleasure more than God will eventually destroy himself and everyone in his wake. The average male fails to understand how his own decisions affect generations to come. Think about yourself and your father situation, and think about your own father's father situation—if there is a void in male leadership, there is a void in your world. The modern slang term is "daddy issues." It applies to fatherless young women too, but this book is really from men, about men, to men.

Societal ills such as crime, poverty, and high incarceration rates are the aftermath of men who embody the 11 traits from 2 Timothy 3:1–4 mentioned above. Can you think of a male over 18 years of age who fits those descriptions? Most grown boys have never been taught how to be responsible or live uprightly—they live for themselves. To make mistakes during the "finding myself" years is human, but to normalize those mistakes is just plain rebellious, primitive, and unbiblical.

How long should the "finding myself" years last? Crackheads are created during these years; homeless kids are created during these years; murderers are created during these years; failed marriages occur during these years. When should a boy stop being a boy and step into manhood? When should his brain chemistry tell him that the old rules of engagement do not apply anymore?

Grown boys have made a conscious decision to relinquish their role as men by choosing money, pleasure, women, and sufficiency independent of God. These four grave errors in judgment have created a void that has compelled women to occupy the role of men. Nature hates a vacuum, but this void has forced women to function as men and fathers. Godly order has been disrupted, so nothing works the way it should. Godly authority has been reversed, so now you know why everything seems backward today. Boys want to be girls; girls want to be boys. Women want to rule the home, and men want to be stay-at-home dad-moms. And men, it's our fault!

We men should be ashamed that we have allowed the enemy to steal our greatest possession, our family! Spiritually indifferent men are responsible for the ambiguity in the minds and hearts of our children. Some place the blame on women, but women are just responding to weak men. Weak men, not weak women, make weak societies. Weak women are usually cast aside and ignored. They are usually left single and childless. And they do not control the direction of a nation. So, we can stop blaming women for what's happening today.

God holds every man responsible for how he leads or fails to lead his family. Fathers, you are accountable for your children. You are also accountable for your wife. If your kids are not behaving, you are the reason why. If they are in jail, you are the reason why. If they are sorry excuses for human beings, you are the reason why. If they are lazy, you are the reason why. If they have no relationship with God, you are the reason why.

Someone must take responsibility for the children, and the man is the God-ordained leader in the family. In Genesis 2:15, God gave Adam instructions to dress the garden of Eden and keep it (KJV). Fathers are in charge of caring for and protecting their families. Fathers are the priests of their homes, and they hold the key to productivity and success in the family.

There is a large family in our town of Brookhaven, Mississippi, and the patriarch took his kids to church every Sunday, taught Bible classes, and showed them how to love God and how to be successful. He modeled how to stay married through his relationship with their mother. He has been married for over 35 years, and all his children are very successful. He took the responsibility on himself to lead his family in the direction of what is good and what is right. This is a great example for men everywhere! When are you, Dad, going to decide to lead your family in the direction of what is right? When will you take your rightful place of leadership?

All men are designed to lead. *All men.* If you are not leading your family, I suggest you ask God to give you the wisdom, knowledge, and understanding of how to lead.

If a person walked into my home library, he would get the wrong idea. He would think I was a horrible father or on the verge of divorce or financial ruin because I have so many books on the subjects of fatherhood, marriage, and finances. But since wisdom is learning from others' mistakes, I constantly read about marriage, fatherhood, and money management because I want to be successful in these areas. What is in your library, Dad? It is time to take back what is yours.

Lack of Accountability

When men are not held accountable for their behavior, their behavior gets worse. Men need accountability.

My father held me accountable. I couldn't get away with anything. And today I appreciate the standards he held me to. There were also very high standards regarding hygiene in our home. If my father could smell your breath, you had to immediately brush your teeth. If he could smell your feet, you had to immediately wash your feet and put foot powder in your shoes. If you were musty, you had to immediately wash under your arms and put deodorant on. He held me accountable to the standard of being a man.

Today, I see countless grown boys with no concept of hygiene. They have no self-awareness, so personal hygiene is foreign to them. Toddlers may have no understanding of personal hygiene, but a young man over the age of 12 should be acutely aware of how he looks and smells. If there were more real men available in their homes, we would not have an entire culture of grown boys who sag their pants, wear earrings, wear their hair like women, and stink.

This is the result of a lack of direction and accountability! The mothers say, "He is just going through a phase." No, he is a child trapped in a man's body.

Men look like men, dress like men, and smell like men. Real men are confident enough in themselves that they do not have to change their look and style to fit in or look cool. Men understand that they do not need earrings, nose rings, sagging pants, or long hair to justify their manhood.

They don't need accessories to impress people. Instead, a man's presence impresses. His accomplishments impress.

When men of renown in the Bible showed up, it was their presence and their manhood that impressed! Their dedication and love for God compelled people to respect and honor them.

Think about Jesus. He did not own a home or have any real possessions, and I don't think He had Facebook or Instagram, but His presence captivated every person He met. Why? He was a real man who lived according to His purpose! He was confident in Himself, and His statement in John 6:38 shows it: "I have come down from heaven, not to do my will, but the will of Him who sent me" (HCSB).

Jesus was accountable to His Father. He did not come as a rogue or rebellious grown boy. He came under the leadership of His Father. He recognized the standards set by God, so He just upheld those standards. He did not try to reinvent the wheel with rebellious desires or misguided intentions. See, if Jesus's lifestyle had been a failure, He could have blamed God.

Accountability gives you layers of checks and balances to help you become successful. And without accountability, success is hard to come by.

I am so glad my daddy taught me the rules of manhood. Many millennial men say the way they dress or look represents their culture and is their personal style. That's childish, and those who say that need to grow up! Showing your skid marks is not culture, it is vulgar and a crime—indecent exposure.

In 2009, Morehouse College (an all-men's college in Atlanta, Georgia) passed a school dress code abolishing sagging pants that revealed undergarments or secondary layers of clothing.[25] The need for this rule screams how

---

25 "More Than Appearances," Inside Higher Ed, October 21, 2009, https://www.insidehighered.com/views/2009/10/22/more-appearances.

far we have gone in the wrong direction. But the policy also reveals that I am not the only one on the bandwagon about the rules of manhood.

I wish law enforcement would arrest people for showing their underwear in public. Some say sagging pants came from the prison lifestyle to advertise you were available. If a woman showed her thong in public, another *woman* would hopefully check her, especially if she had small boys around. She would not be allowed in most places of business, and someone would eventually call the police. So why do we let men get away with this crime?

Real men are very aware of how personal bodily decisions can affect their success. Long hair is popular among some males, especially rock-and-roll groups.

Long hair for some is their personal style, but my concern is what style God wants me to wear. What is His standard for me in my appearance as a man? We are talking about being a man, not being someone who is confused and trying to impress people he doesn't even know. According to 1 Corinthians 11:14, long hair is not manly because it dishonors the man's essence. It dishonors his manhood.

Sadly, there is no initiation process in America for boys to pass into manhood. Grown boys are males who never graduated into manhood, despite being over the age of 18. King David from the Bible told his successor and son, Solomon, in 1 Kings 2:2, "Be strong, therefore, and prove yourself a man" (NKJV). If every father would challenge his sons to prove themselves, we would have a different culture of men.

I have never been to jail, never smoked marijuana, and never been arrested, and I have no kids outside my marriage. I am not perfect by any means, but my manly foundation is firm because of my dad and my relationship with God. Good fathers hold their kids accountable. Just being there communicates, "I am watching you, and if you get out of line, there will be negative consequences. But if you do good, there will be good consequences too!"

When I reached puberty and my voice got deep, my father reminded me that I could sass my teachers or my mother if I wanted to, but I would have to answer to him when it was all over. That set the tone because I did not want to answer to that man!

A big reason for the healthy fear I had of my father was the consequences of getting out of line. The healthy fear was just respect and honor for the man we called Dad. I'll never forget the last whipping he gave me, when I was 14. My "babysitter mom" told me to get the mail from the mailbox, but I told her I would go after it stopped raining. Well, she told Dad. I am not sure what she said, but all he heard was that I had refused to get the mail. He found a large stick and let me have it. Yes, corporal punishment was a real thing back in the day. I did not realize that would be my last whipping, but I am glad it was! Corporal punishment doesn't make people violent—it makes us disciplined.

Dad was tough when I needed it, but on the flip side, if I needed anything for school, band, football, fishing, hunting, or camping, he made sure I had it. If I needed a tutor, he would tutor me or get someone else to help. If the power went out, he made sure the wood stove was hot so we could cook and heat up water to take baths. That's what dads do—they bring security and stability to the family!

Being a father is a blessing. All the absentee dads have missed out on one of the greatest calls of life—*fatherhood.* It is a godly role and must not be taken lightly. Without my dad, I would have been rebellious and destructive to myself and society. I would probably have earrings in my ear, tattoos all over my body, and a drinking problem. Without my father, I would likely have had several kids with several different women and a lot of baby mama drama. I am grateful for a man who understood true manhood and recognized I would not be a boy forever.

I have embraced fatherhood in my own home with my two sons. I tried to be balanced and fair in my parenting and hold them accountable. My sons are both in college now, and they love me *(I think)*, their mom, and God. They often tell me what a great childhood they had and how grateful they are to have had a dad in the home. That makes me proud! It makes me prouder than anything else I have accomplished in my life. It's an achievement worth bragging about to bring two boys into this world and ultimately make them better men than me. That was always my goal, to make them better men.

When you die, man, will you have left a legacy on this earth better than you? Or will you have neglected your responsibilities as a father and left this world worse than when you came? Every absentee father and grown boy leaves the world worse than they found it.

I always told my wife when our boys were small that we are not raising boys, we are raising men. Despite what anyone thinks, fathers matter. Fathers can do what mothers can't. When Dad says something, everyone listens. When Mom says something, everyone hears. Dads have the power to hold their kids accountable.

In the introduction to this book, we discussed the delinquent elephants of Africa. The moral of the story is that even the animal kingdom knows the importance of male modeling and accountability. Why is it so difficult for men and women to understand this? I thought men and women were the higher-level thinkers among all living creatures. Why do we think prosperity and freedom excuse us from responsibility to God and family? Prosperity and freedom will never excuse us from our social roles in society and our responsibility to our Creator.

To create a child and refuse to take care of that child and hold that child accountable is less than animal like. It's savage.

Lack of Emotional Understanding

Rejection creates an emotional laceration in the soul of a child. Deficits of wisdom, knowledge, and understanding have destroyed more people than just plain rebellion. According to Proverbs 4:7, "Wisdom is the principal thing; therefore get wisdom: and with all thy getting get understanding" (KJV). Lack of understanding about how rejection affects a child is another source of the problem.

A 15-year-old boy I knew, Carlos (not his real name), committed suicide several years ago. He was an amazing kid, athletic and handsome with a great future ahead of him, who would hang out with my sons and come to sleepovers and birthday parties, but in a moment of weakness, he decided to end it all. His parents divorced, and his mom remarried. He felt like an outcast, and after two previous suicide attempts, he finally succeeded. I was very disappointed and hurt because he had so much potential. Why did he do it? Because he felt rejected. And that's how powerful rejection can be, powerful enough to lead someone to take his own life.

To be rejected means to be cast aside, cast off, or cast away—to be thrown away as having no value.[26] Rejection makes us feel useless, abandoned, and worthless. No doubt Carlos felt this way. He was angry over the divorce, and although a breakup with his girlfriend was the straw that broke the camel's back, it was not the underlying issue. Anger usually comes from four main sources: hurt, fear, frustration, and unfair treatment. Carlos was probably hurt from the divorce, fearful about the future, and frustrated about everything.

---

26 *Merriam-Webster*, "rejected," accessed July 1, 2025, https://www.merriam-webster.com/dictionary/rejected.

The number one risk factor for suicide among young men is fatherlessness.[27] It is a colossal failure to treat relationships, marriage, and children with blatant disregard because the success of society depends on the success of our families!

The strength of the family is a marker of a successful society. A study on marriage and relationships by Michael Rosenfeld from Stanford University concluded that approximately 69% of divorces are initiated by women.[28] According to USA Today, only 41% of first marriages end in divorce. The same article says 60% of second marriages and 73% of third marriages end in divorce.[29] Do we have an excess of unhappy, unfulfilled, selfish women who cannot understand how one decision affects an entire generation? A better question is what leads to these breakups.

Most likely, there is a weak man allowing spiritual and emotional trickery to take root in the heart of his family. He is unprepared to lead and ill-qualified to run the major corporation called family, so it is easier to end the marriage than fix deficiencies. Leave at the first sign of trouble. Marriage is difficult, and every strong marriage has gone through the fire. Divorce is not always the correct solution. Most marriages could survive with enough love and maturity on both sides.

We will never see Carlos graduate high school, graduate college, get married, have kids, or live in the pursuit of happiness. We don't know whether he would have found the cure for HIV or cancer, or would have created the next Amazon. We don't know whether he could have been the guy to lead America into the promised land. And now we'll never know!

---

27 Farrell and Grey, *Boy Crisis.*

28 Michael J. Rosenfeld, "Who Wants the Breakup? Gender and Breakup in Heterosexual Couples," in *Social Networks and the Life Course: Integrating the Development of Human Lives and Social Relational Networks*, eds. Duane F. Alwin, Diane Felmlee, and Derek Kreager (Springer, 2018), 221–43.

29 Daryl Austin, "Divorce Rates Are Trickier to Pin Down Than You May Think. Here's Why," USA Today, last updated October 2, 2024, https://www.usatoday.com/story/life/health-wellness/2024/09/05/marriage-divorce-rate/74899214007.

I don't know the circumstances of Carlos's parents' divorce, but if we could roll back the hands of time, I wonder whether they would choose differently. Could they comprehend how rejection would eventually destroy his future? Children in their formative years need all the assurance, nurturing, love, affection, and direction possible to weather the battles that come with life. Divorce disrupts children's normal emotional development, and absentee fathers compound these emotional wounds.

I met a guy today whose parents divorced when he was small. He says he never went to the same school district two years consecutively. He is anxious and clearly has some sexual identity issues. Wounded souls wound. Hurt people hurt people. Ignorance to the social, emotional, and spiritual ramifications of fatherlessness got us here. So, we must backtrack to ground zero and start over in the parenting and relationship arenas.

When you have a child (whether you are married or not), your life is no longer about you. Your life will never be the same, and it behooves you to make life about your child. Isn't that what our heavenly Father does for us? Having sex and children within the confines of marriage is the best scenario. Once you become a parent, you are not the center of the universe anymore. Everything revolves around your child, and if you cannot comprehend that fact, you should remain childless.

Wouldn't it be great if all the potential deadbeat dads remained childless? Maybe the government should subsidize vasectomies for all the men who clearly do not want kids and clearly do not have the means to care for another human being. I would vote for this law and send in the first $1,000. Would it be cruel and inhumane? Well, let's ask all the fatherless kids in our community that we mentor whether it was cruel and inhumane for their sperm donor dads to sire children for several women and never be involved in their lives.

We have several children at our church who have only seen their fathers on Facebook. Their fathers have *never* been involved in their lives. A few kids that we mentor wouldn't even know their fathers if they walked up to them. Absentee fathers like this do not deserve children. Our concern should be for the children. Children are the focal point of a man's life if he is a father.

Real men do not run from responsibility. "My kids' mom is crazy," some dads say. Well, Dad, wasn't she crazy when you had sex with her? If she is crazy, what does that say about you? You attract what you are. Why would you have a child with a crazy woman? That means you are really the crazy one! They say that birds of a feather flock together. Stop making excuses. Blame helps no one when a child is involved.

Parenting is complicated and hard. It will be your most difficult job ever! But let's remember, there are no illegitimate children, only illegitimate parents. Children do not ask to be here. They are brought here by their parents.

My mom would tell my sisters and me, "Kids come from Timbuktu, and if you are not ready for a child—leave them there." This quote was her way of telling us not to bring any out-of-wedlock kids into this world.

So, if you say your child was an accident or surprise, you are lying to yourself. Your child is not an accident or a surprise. Your child has a divine appointment to be here at this juncture in time. Scripture agrees with this statement, as described here in Jeremiah 1:5: "Before I formed thee in the belly I knew thee; and before thou camest forth out of the womb I sanctified thee" (KJV). God knew that child would be here, and He knew what his name would be. The circumstances surrounding his conception may not be ideal, but God knew it was time. So, get over the excuses and be responsible for what you created.

Some dads will say, "I am not sure whether the child is mine." Well, with DNA testing, this issue is no longer a problem. It costs about $100 to find out whether a child is yours or not, so don't inadvertently take care of another man's child—unless you choose to. A family friend, Mr. Mance Ravencraft, would always say, "Many men have rocked another man's baby." Before DNA testing, this statement was true, but today, science has caught up with infidelity.

Understanding is what we need today in the minds and hearts of the parents birthing children. Kids are not born dropouts, drug heads, gang-bangers, or murderers. They are conditioned to be this way by the environments they are nurtured in.

I have never met a child who says, "I want to spend twenty-five to life in prison," "I want to spend my whole life in addiction programs," or "I want to live in poverty." If every parent could simply understand what happens in a dysfunctional, incomplete family, we could change the way we approach dating, relationships, and parenting. Women would look beyond the basics in men and would search for integrity, morals, strength, and parenting skills. Men would look for women who are feminine and submissive and who cherish their purity and value.

We need women of value mothering the next generation of children, and we need mighty men parenting that generation.

If America falls victim to the hands of another country, the reasons will be obvious: moral and spiritual erosion, combined with internal division and strife. Advice to all world superpowers: If you want to destroy America, encourage further dissolution of the American family, encourage gender identity crises, and keep the man out of the home. At some point, we will not have enough *real men* to fight.

Remember, real men run *to* danger. Real men stand and fight for their families and their country. Real men fight for what is right.

The following passage is from the article "39 Years Ago, a KGB Defector Chillingly Predicted Modern America," discussing G. Edward Griffin's interview with Yuri Bezmenov, propagandist for the KGB.

> In 1984, [KGB defector Yuri] Bezmenov gave an interview to G. Edward Griffin [on the Russian strategy designed to destroy America]…[He said] most of the work, 85% of it, was "a slow process which we call either ideological subversion, active measures, or psychological warfare."
>
> …Here's how he further defined ideological subversion:
>
> "What it basically means is: to change the perception of reality of every American to such an extent that despite the abundance of information no one is able to come to sensible conclusions in the interest of defending themselves, their families, their community, and their country."
>
> Bezmenov described this process as "a great brainwashing" that has four basic stages. The first stage is called "demoralization" which takes from 15 to 20 years to achieve.…That is the minimum number of years it takes to re-educate one generation of students.…
>
> "A person who was demoralized is unable to assess true information. The facts tell nothing to him. Even if I shower him with information, with authentic proof, with documents, with pictures; even if I take him by force to the Soviet Union and show him [a] concentration camp, he will refuse to believe it, until he [receives] a kick in his fan-bottom."[30]

30 Paul Ratner, "Thirty-Nine Years Ago, A KGB Defector Chillingly Predicted Modern America," Big Think, January 13, 2023, https://bigthink.com/the-present/yuri-bezmenov.

If you will notice, America has become like this, with many people like Black Lives Matter rejecting facts in favor of opinion. Emotions matter more than facts in most of these social organizations.

> Once demoralization is completed, the second stage of ideological brainwashing is "destabilization." [Destabilization is a psychological technique used in brainwashing and abuse to disorient and disarm a victim. It can involve failing to acknowledge good work, assigning meaningless tasks, removing areas of responsibility without consultation, repeatedly reminding the victim of mistakes, setting the victim up to fail, and persistent attempts to demoralize the victim.]... The third stage would be "crisis." It would take up to six weeks to send a country into crisis.... The crisis would bring a "violent change of power, structure, and economy" and will be followed by the last stage, "normalization." That's when your country is basically taken over, living under a new ideology and reality.
>
> ...This will happen to America unless it gets rid of people who will bring it to a crisis, warned Bezmenov. What's more, "If people will fail to grasp the impending danger of that development, nothing ever can help [the] United States," adding, "You may kiss goodbye to your freedom."
>
> ...In another somewhat terrifying excerpt, here's what Bezmenov had to say about what is really happening in the United States: It may think it is living in peace, but it has been actively at war with Russia, and for some time:
>
> "Most of the American politicians, media, and educational system trains another generation of people who think they are living at the peacetime," said the former KGB agent. "False. United States is in a state of war: undeclared, total war against the basic principles and foundations of this system."[31]

---

31 Ratner, "KGB Defector Chillingly Predicted."

Know Your Enemy

I am not very political, but any formidable opponent studies and learns his enemy. He develops ways to undermine the basic values and principles that shape his enemy's livelihood. Our real enemy is not Russia, it is satan! His ultimate goal is to destroy the family by destroying the head of the family, the men.

All vices target men. Drugs target men. Alcohol targets men. Promiscuity, porn, and illicit sex target men. Greed targets men. Fame targets men. If you really want to know how much integrity a man has, provide him with unlimited access to power, money, and women. You will quickly find out who that man really is.

Our real enemy is not racism, poverty, or crime—it is the father of lies. He wants to steal your strength, kill your hopes, destroy your dreams. And we know this to be true because Mark 3:27 confirms, "No man can enter into a strong man's house, and spoil his goods, except he will first bind the strong man; and then he will spoil his house" (KJV). Satan targets men with a relentless ferocity because he understands men are the strength of their communities, so he must eliminate the strong man of the house.

How many of you are aware of how much the devil wants to destroy you, your family, and your children? Are you aware of how he eases in unannounced through any crack in your armor?

All is fair in love and war. This is war—spiritual warfare—and the family is losing! America is losing—it is on the verge of complete failure because of family disintegration. We have a great military power, a great economy, but all this will fail when the conspiracy to end family values is complete. The only question now is whether you will fight for your future, your kids' future, or watch it be taken from you.

Real men are willing to die for their convictions. Real men know that immorality weakens the fortitude of any nation. Once there is no fortitude, we become a weak, limp-wristed nation caught up in conjecture, false narratives, and deception. The Achilles' heel of any country is immorality and weak men.

Poor leadership comes quickly after the first two. Immorality and weak men will destroy any family of people—irrespective of race, creed, background, or economic status. It may take weeks, months, years, decades, or generations. Nevertheless, destruction is final. Immorality and weak men invite curses into their world, without any sense of responsibility for this spiritual suicide.

The enemy comes to steal, kill, and destroy, according to John 10:10. We are in a perpetual state of war for our families and for the next generation. I want to convey full understanding of the problem. Professionals seem to evade the underlying problem of family disintegration and weak malehood. But this problem stares you in the face daily, regardless of your profession.

Now, I am not a male chauvinist by any means. My mom is a woman, my three sisters are women, and my wife is a woman, and I love them all. But I do have God and history on my side. Strong men make strong families, strong families make strong communities, strong communities make strong cities, strong cities make strong states, and strong states make strong nations. That's just the way reality works.

For all the feminists out there, look in *your* neighborhood or place of business, and make an honest assessment of the families who are considered strong. In most cases, there is a strong man at the helm. He is not the boss—he is really a servant to his family. He is at the bottom serving, undergirding his family—which is what he is supposed to do.

A strong father will make a family strong. He is selfless and willing to undergo any trial to ensure the stability and longevity of his family. He takes the family on his back and leads with a servant's heart.

A woman would be out of her mind to not want a man like this. If I were a woman, I would want a man like this. Strong men make strong nations. Strong men with strong women make even stronger nations. Both are necessary if strength and resilience are to be imparted to the child. *Both.*

Understanding human nature and the emotional consequences of bad family dynamics is our goal as people. Bears understand bears, so if you try to harm a bear cub, the mother bear will maul you to death and eat you. What if all human parents were like mother bears? Pedophilia and child sex trafficking would stop overnight. I wish parents, especially fathers, would protect our children like animals protect their offspring. I hope we have enough emotional understanding of our roles as parents to lead, guide, and teach the next generation in the ways of God.

Government Policies: How Did We Get Here?

In the 1960s, welfare reform intended to eliminate poverty in America. It was a lofty goal, but in John 12:8, Jesus Christ says, "For the poor always ye have with you" (KJV). Fast-forward the clock 2,000 years after Jesus said that, and the poor are still with us. Even though there are over 3,000 billionaires in the world,[32] we still have poor people all over the world.

The public welfare amendments of 1962 further subsidized the lives of poor Americans, but there was a catch. What was the catch? You could not have a man in the home. According to the documentary *Chicago at the Crossroad*, "The government would not pay for a child who had a father

32 "World's Billionaires List," *Forbes*, accessed July 1, 2025, https://www.forbes.com/billionaires.

living with that child."[33] This little statement compelled poor mothers to marry the government instead of their men.

I appreciate our government and pray for our leaders, but I do not have confidence in them like I have confidence in God. As a matter of fact, Jeremiah 17:5 says that you are cursed if you put your trust in man. I believe that God's pattern for the family is the best since the existence of mankind.

God's plan is to create a culture centered around Him. Feeding people does not create godly culture; providing low-income housing does not create godly culture; providing cheap medical insurance does not create godly culture. God's plan is to create families where physical, emotional, and spiritual growth takes place. God wants to indoctrinate people with Kingdom-mindedness, not America-mindedness. He wants us to depend on Him, not the government. The government becomes your god if you place all of your faith and hope in it for sustenance.

Government assistance was designed to help you when you are in a financially tough position. However, once you recover, your benefits should go to someone else. Believe it or not, I was once on government assistance.

My oldest son, Matthew, was born when I was in medical school, so we had Medicaid and food subsidies at that time. I was not ashamed because I knew this was just a small handup, not a handout. My plan was to terminate the subsidies as soon as possible, and we did after a year or two. Now there are several local families near us who live in government housing and get food and insurance subsidies. This assistance is fine for a short time, but these particular families have been on it for three generations.

---

33 *Chicago at the Crossroad*, directed by Brian Schodorf (Schodorf Media Creative, 2019).

God wants to indoctrinate "love, joy, peace, longsuffering, gentleness, goodness, faith, meekness, [and] temperance," which are the fruits of His Spirit, as outlined in Galatians 5:22–23 (KJV). He does not want to just feed you. If he just feeds you, then you will get fat and lazy. Government policies do not work when they make you fat and lazy and disincentivize ambition.

The U.S. government essentially alienated the father's role as provider and eliminated him from the home. This great experiment has had enough time to fully manifest itself, and 59 years later, we see the results. But what you see in your daily news was predicted by Senator Daniel Patrick Moynihan (assistant secretary of labor under President Johnson and later senator in New York) in 1965 in the Moynihan Report.

He said that the rise in Black single-mother families was caused not by a lack of jobs but by a destructive vein in ghetto culture that could be traced to slavery times and continued discrimination in the American South under Jim Crow. The report concluded that the high rate of single-mother families would devastate and hinder progress of Blacks toward economic and political equality.

This report was criticized by liberals at the time, and Moynihan was called racist. He reports that "The steady expansion of…public assistance programs in general, can be taken as a measure of the **steady disintegration of the Negro family structure** over the past generation in the United States."[34] He also noticed that the rates of Black male unemployment and welfare enrollment, instead of running parallel as they always had, started to diverge in 1962 in a way that would come to be called "Moynihan's scissors."

34 Daniel Patrick Moynihan, *The Negro Family: The Case for National Action* (Office of Policy Planning and Research, United States Department of Labor, 1965), 14.

RECREATION OF MOYNIHAN'S SCISSORS GRAPH

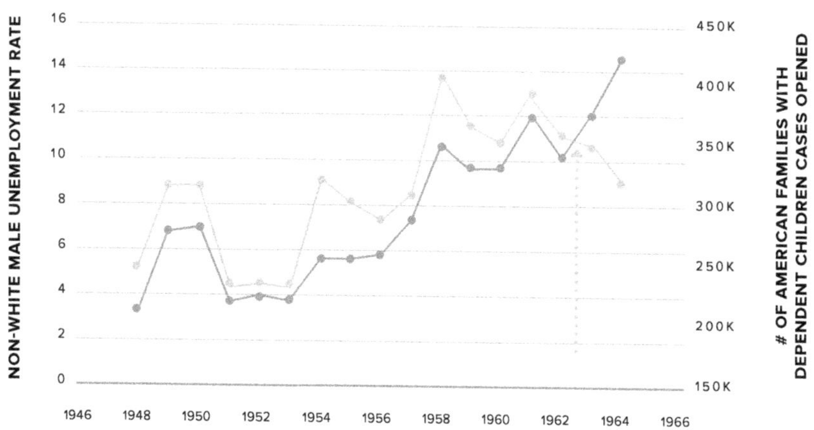

Data from U.S. Department of Labor, "The Moynihan Report: An Annotated Edition," *The Atlantic*, September 14, 2015, https://www.theatlantic.com/politics/archive/2015/09/the-moynihan-report-an-annotated-edition/404632/.

Since 1948, as nonwhite male unemployment rose, more mothers and families enrolled in welfare. However, after 1962, this parallel ended, and the mothers' and families' needs for assistance were unattached and incongruent with rates of nonwhite male unemployment. Despite nonwhite men being employed, the mothers and families continued to enroll in welfare programs.

Dads' economic support was no longer needed in the home, so mothers depended on the government despite having men who were gainfully employed. This divergence and separation of the man from his family alienated the greatest influence on the family. This alienation has been perpetuated over the course of five decades, and we no longer need suppositions or estimations of the outcome. We know. It failed and created the epidemic of fatherlessness we see today.

Brookings.edu reported that, in 1965, 24% of Black infants and 3.1% of white infants were born to single mothers. By 1990, the rates had risen to 64% for Black infants and 18% for whites.[35] In 2020, the National Vital Statistics Reports states the following percentages of infants born to single mothers: 69.4% for Black infants, 68.2% for American Indians/Alaska Natives, 50.4% for Native Hawaiians/other Pacific Islanders, 51.8% for Hispanics, 28.2% for whites, and 11.7% for Asian Americans.[36]

So, this rise from 24% to 69% in illegitimate births in Blacks has created a fatherless community. The welfare amendments mentioned earlier insidiously pushed fathers out of the home. Mothers fed their children, but at the expense of the most important men in their children's lives, their dads.

A fatherless society is a crime-ridden, poverty-ridden, immorality-ridden cesspool of a world. America fits this bill. Government policies should always help, but they did not help in this case. The whole program achieved the opposite of its intentions! What word would you use for policies that did the exact opposite of their intention? Backward? Dumb? Insane?

Think with me: Fatherlessness is one of the greatest predictors of poverty, but welfare reform created more fatherlessness. How could we be so naive? Are we that ignorant? Only one man had the audacity to acknowledge the fallacies in these governmental policies. Welfare will not end poverty—it perpetuates it. Government policy tried to end homelessness, but the main demographic of homeless children and runaways is kids growing up in homes without fathers.[37] So, was Senator Moynihan correct in his conclusions? Yes. The statistics we discuss in this book prove his prophesy.

Welfare reform compelled Black and poor women to marry the government. This union would be a match made in heaven if the government would help your daughter with her homework every day, take your

35 George A. Akerlof and Janet L. Yellen, "An Analysis of Out-of-wedlock Births in the United States," Brookings, August 1, 1996, https://www.brookings.edu/articles/an-analysis-of-out-of-wedlock-births-in-the-united-states.

36 Martin et al., "Births."

37 "Thirty-Six Shocking Statistics."

son fishing, cook when Mom is tired, take the kids to guitar practice, play catch with the boys, and tell your children "I love you." We know these intimate moments will never happen when the government is acting as father.

Finally, tell me who is going to lead that family in the ways of God if Daddy is the government? Who is going to teach weekly Bible studies? Who is going to lead prayer every night before bedtime? Who is going to love Mom? Despite the government wanting to play Dad, it can never be a daddy to a child. Fatherhood is a divine calling—not sperm donation.

One single mother who has four kids says her kids' fathers are only sperm donors. Is that what you are? If you call yourself a man but you are only known for sperm donation, you are not a man. You are a grown boy.

The role of father is a godly role, and many modern women and men cannot comprehend this fact. No one can replace the father in the home. *No one.* Coaches can't. Pastors can't. Teachers can't. Mentors can't. The government sure can't. Not even a stepdad can be what a biological dad can be. No formula replaces God's formula for the family. These replacements can function as surrogates, but they cannot fully occupy the role of a child's daddy.

How did we get here? Does sex feel better today than it did 60 years ago? Are the women prettier than the women 60 years ago? Are more of the men hunks and studs or better in bed compared to 60 years ago? The answer to all these questions is *no*. Our morals changed. Our approach to sex, parenting, and family changed.

My wife and I had our sons before we were married, so this change in thinking took place in me too. No one is exempt from the effects of immorality and "do what makes you feel good" mentality. Thank God we worked through our differences and got married.

In case you are wondering, I was the problem. I was immature and broken, and I did not know the value of bringing another human being into this world. I was exposed to pornography at a young age, and it warped my thinking. It created broken relationship and intimacy mechanics that almost destroyed me. That is what the enemy wanted for me, but God said otherwise. I am still here, and the enemy could not destroy what God purposed in me. All males must grow up as I did. Every grown boy can become a man when he decides to.

Who's Your Daddy?

In Psalms 68:5, God says He will be "a father to the fatherless" (NIV). Only God can truly fulfill the role of father. Only God can love a child like that child needs to be loved, whether the dad is present or absent. Even spiritually, we are disillusioned, and we lack purpose when we do not know our heavenly Father.

The Lord's Prayer starts out with "Our Father which art in Heaven" (Matthew 6:9, KJV). The first two words of this prayer completely acknowledge "I belong," "I am needed," "I am a part of a family," "I have a dad," "I know Him," and "He knows me." These proclamations give strength to the heart of a child. They give confidence. They give direction and personal responsibility to live up to the expectations of a father.

A government could never come close to giving a child what he needs. Food, housing, and insurance benefits are secondary to love, quality time, support, and sincere concern. Yes, food and housing are basic needs, but if a man loves his family, he will guarantee these are provided for, to his own detriment.

Let's look at the life of a woman married to the government compared to the life of a woman married to a man. Let's talk about my wife, Joy. The government could not come close to taking care of her like I take care of her. You should see the car she drives (and how clean it is) and the house she lives in. I love her, so I guarantee you that she will *always* live a well-taken-care-of life. I even keep her gas tank full, so she rarely goes to the gas station. I run her bathwater almost every night, and I even cook sometimes. And I can't cook!

And if I die prematurely, she will be set financially for life. I am probably worth more dead than alive. That's love, if you ask me. Do you honestly think any government would go to those lengths for her? They don't even know her name—except at tax time.

Love goes beyond welfare. Love goes beyond living arrangements. Love provides. Love gives. "You can give without love, but you cannot love without giving," says Gavin Gatlin, a member of our church youth group. Love is why we must get the father back in the home. This grand experiment to eliminate poverty has failed poor people, failed Black people, and failed America. Unrestricted, unqualified welfare is a recipe for disaster.

If we want to decrease poverty, crime, homelessness, high school dropouts, suicides, behavioral disorders, substance abuse, rape, and obesity, here is a novel approach: Encourage marriage before sex. Encourage marriage before bringing another life into this world. Let's get back to the days when having kids out of wedlock was taboo, when sex before marriage was taboo.

Maybe I am out of date, but the statistics I have shared are not out of date, and the Bible will never be out of date. Sex is powerful, and if done with the wrong person, it creates long-lasting consequences. We know what happens to a society without men in the home. That society is America. We know what happens to families led by women only. We know what happens to kids without fathers in the home.

If you are not convinced of the importance of having a father in the home, then look at the people in your community. Look at the homes that have both a father and mother present compared to homes where there is only a mother present. Compare and contrast the differences in lifestyle, health, wealth, and sense of purpose.

If you came to Brookhaven, I could take you to areas where many families are made up of just mothers and kids, then take you to areas where most families are fathers, mothers, and kids, so you could make your own real-life assessment of the facts I am presenting. Observe those single-mother homes over time. Observe their kids. Observe their grandkids. Observe their great-grandkids. Are there exceptions? Yes, but the nuclear family has been a powerful entity since the beginning of time. We call it the "nuclear" family because it is powerful financially, socially, and spiritually.

Prior to the 1960s, Blacks had social wealth, but when social wealth failed, all other sources of wealth suffered. Fast-forward the clock to today, and we see the results of a disintegrated family unit.

These statistics apply to other ethnicities as well, but because the Black community is a minority, small changes yield huge consequences. Small changes in family structure are magnified within the confines of a minority population. However, an out-of-wedlock birth rate of 69% in the Black community is not small! It is enormous!

The enemy has almost completely sealed the fate of an entire community by removing the father from the home. If you still disagree, evaluate the young men in your workplace, church, and community who did not have fathers in their homes. Evaluate their discipline, direction, confidence, and identity. Evaluate the young ladies who grew up fatherless. Scale them on health, confidence, emotional stability, and desire for male companionship.

Families led by men alone do not suffer the same ill effects that families led by women alone do. A mindset change has taken place in the minds and hearts of modern society, and the government is complicit in this shift—if not liable. The current mindset says, "It is OK to have children out of wedlock" or "I don't need a man."

I recently went fishing at Toledo Bend Reservoir in Many, Louisiana, and a young lady at a local restaurant took my order. I asked her about her life goals and her plans after high school. Then I asked her if she had any kids. She said yes, and I asked about the father. She said, "I don't need him. I can do it all by myself."

These statements prove my case and break my heart. She was 16 or 17 years old, working, and taking care of a child while she was still a child herself! Where was her dad? Where was her mom? Where was her pastor? Where were her community leaders? Where was that baby's father?

My suggestion for welfare in America would be a few years of assistance with vocational/degree training as a corequirement for that assistance. Mandatory DNA tests would be given for paternity, and mandatory child support benefits would be initiated based on state child support laws.

Every child would receive support from the father, even if his employer paid him in cash. Employers who paid in cash would be placed on notice that their employee had wage garnishment for child support benefits.

Negative drug tests would be part of the inclusion criteria. Food and housing benefits would get cut by 25% each year. Educational and vocational training would be provided during this time frame so that, after four years, the mother could have earned a bachelor's, vocational, or associate's degree.

After four years, all benefits would stop. If the mother did not complete her bachelor's, vocational, or associate's degree, she would be placed in job-training programs. If, during the four years, she had another child at any time after the birth of the first, she would be required to work to keep the benefits active. Women with only one child would not be required to work, as long as they were in the vocational/degree-training program.

Government daycare would be a part of this program to help care for kids while the mother was in school or job training. Mandatory birth control would be provided to these women to prevent further unwanted pregnancies during the program. Ideally, the women should be married since God expects us to be married prior to any sexual activity but they are obviously sexually active, considering they are mothers. If the mothers could not comply with the mandates of the program, then they would be taken out of the program. They could get jobs or starve. They could also consider marrying their children's fathers.

Programs like this incentivize people to find employment, get educations or vocations, take care of their own families, get married, and find purpose in life. Does that sound cruel and inhumane? What's greater than finding purpose in life? Nothing.

Marriage courses would be mandatory as part of the program so that the women could be taught the benefits of being wives and could learn how to be good wives. Women who were currently on government assistance when the program was initiated would be given four years to complete degrees, vocational school, or specialized job training.

If you disagree with my plan, then please design a better one. Our goal is to build strong families—not weak, uneducated, drugged-out, homeless, incarcerated, broke people!

Go to the ghetto. You usually see uneducated, drugged-out, homeless, impoverished people who hate their lives. But they have no clue how to get out of the rut they are in. We want to get people out of poverty—not leave them there! You may disagree with my choice of words, but we are offering solutions!

Our goal is to please God, build people up, and create strong families. Strong-minded people create their own sufficiency. No program will be perfect, but we must start where we are with what we have. We must open our minds to understand that the current system has stressed our single mothers, relinquished the responsibility of the fathers, and failed our kids. If an entire culture of people is dependent on the government, then that government has complete control. And no one deserves complete control over your life!

God does not even demand complete control over you. Current government programs discourage the poor and perpetuate the obvious prevalence of single-mother-led homes with no real solution to end poverty.

This solution will work. It will decrease benefits over time so single mothers can stop making a career out of motherhood alone. Our goal is to totally eliminate the need for TANF (Temporary Assistance for Needy Families) and increase the number of women who marry before having children. We want to give people purpose and legitimate opportunity to be successful in life. We also want to build strong families, which will build a strong nation. It behooves any woman who wants to have kids to marry so that she is entitled to alimony, child support, and whatever else the law allows.

Lack of Spiritual Leadership in the Community

The Black church has failed Black America. Why? Sixty-nine percent of Black babies are born out of wedlock.[38] This stat illustrates the number one problem in America as a whole, and Black churches have failed to lead their members in the ways of God. They have led them in the ways of modernism, sports fanaticism, materialism, and pleasure, but they have failed God and their communities in spiritual leadership.

---

38 Martin et al., "Births."

God expects His anointed men and women to teach the Bible and encourage people to study, read, and engage with biblical principles for living. This process was neglected over the last two to three generations, so now we see a new generation of young people with no moral compass.

When a person has no moral compass, that person has no internal governor or conscience to weather the storms of life. Individuals without a deeply embedded moral destination find themselves shipwrecked on the waves of life.

Our spiritual leaders missed the mark and will be held accountable for their passivity. Real men of God ignore popular culture and preach godly culture. We have tons of preachers, but real men of God are rare. Godly culture does not flaunt flashy, worldly lifestyles. Godly culture recognizes sin as shameful, as something that should be avoided at all costs.

Yes, fornication is a sin according to the Bible. 1 Corinthians 6:18–19 says, “Flee fornication. Every sin that a man doeth is without the body; but he that committeth fornication sinneth against his own body. What? know ye not that your body is the temple of the Holy Ghost which is in you, which ye have of God, and ye are not your own?” (KJV). If anyone has sex outside the confines of marriage, that person sins against their own body!

Sex *feels* good, but it may not *be* good if done at the wrong time. Timing is everything with God, including when it comes to sex. Mistimed sexual activity has created a curse in the Black community because we have circumvented God’s way with our own way. God designed sex for us to enjoy within a marriage, and it is one of the best things you do within marriage.

The enemy has cheapened sex so much that modern culture has no standard regarding sex. “If it feels good, do it” is what we hear today in some circles. God’s standard is *the* standard, but this idea seems old-fashioned and simpleminded.

But isn't sex love? No. If sex were love, then prostitutes would be the most loved people in the world. Quite the contrary, because they are unloved—they cheapen the value of their bodies. Because they have been rejected time and time again, they feel unloved. Women who love their bodies do not carelessly experiment with them.

One abnormal sex act could destroy a person's entire life. If I had sex with the wrong person, I could lose my marriage, family, medical license, income, ministry, and all my dreams. However, I could embezzle money or commit insurance fraud, and I would not have to register as a sex offender, and there is a slight possibility that I could practice medicine again. My family would love me through the process, and hopefully I would not lose my ministry. But illicit sex would bring a curse into my world. That is how powerful sex is!

These conversations are the conversations every God-ordained leader should be having with everyone in their circles of influence. All parents should also be having these conversations with their children. Godly principles protect you, just like speed limits and seat belts protect you. Godly rules protect us from unintended consequences.

Right now, I am taking care of a patient who is in the hospital. She had four children before she was 21. She had her first when she was 14. She is in her 30s now, but her 18-year-old son was murdered about a year and a half ago. Her other son is in prison, and her daughter (age 14) just had a child. Her kids, when they were small, were removed from her home due to lack of resources. She is severely depressed, on dialysis, and wants to die.

Was the sex that good? I don't think so. Were five minutes of pleasure worth a lifetime of pain? Our current culture has chosen the pleasures of sin for a season. We must wake up!

Frankly, Black people will be an extinct population if the foolishness and disobedience continue. Maybe this was the original plan. Godly instruction gives a person the spiritual fortitude to navigate the land mines of life. Wisdom forces you to learn from the past and live in the present, and it prepares you for the future.

Having the wrong sex can destroy you. I challenge you to take a single mother to lunch and discuss the struggles she has had with raising kids alone. Ask her how difficult it is to cook, do homework, take the kids to football practice, do laundry, comb hair, iron, and discipline, all alone. Ask her how hard it is to care for a sick child when she is sick too. Ask her how much it hurts her to tell her kids they can't go to church camp or basketball camp due to lack of money. Ask her how much it hurts when she finds out her 15-year-old daughter is pregnant. The cycle continues.

Check out this conversation (monologue) my wife had over text with this single mother.

> I just needed somebody that doesn't know me to hear my story. I don't want anything. I just wanna be able to express myself. Honestly, I don't know what to do, and I just want somebody else to tell me it's OK to feel the way I do.
>
> As you know, I am a momma of four kids. I don't know where I ever went wrong. I tried my whole life to do what any mother would do and be there. I gave up my whole life for this moment to give my kids a life I didn't have growing up. No, I haven't been a perfect mother, but I always keep a roof and clean house, clothes on their back and work myself to death, so they won't ever go without.
>
> As a mother I gave this life all I got, but sometimes I do fall short. But I am doing it by myself, and I never looked for [nobody] to help me 'cause these are my kids. I [be] depressed on

so many days, not because I'm not happy with life, but I know my kids deserve more. I know there are times I wanna go all out but trying to keep a roof over our head. Sometimes I gotta pick between paying a bill and getting my boys' hair cut or not eating at work, so I can save money for the lil simple things they ask for.

Today I actually woke up feeling like it would be a good day, but got into it with my kids' dads. But I am beefing with his girlfriend—like sometimes I don't understand people. I don't bother nobody. I let him be a parent whenever he wants to, but I can't take it no more. I been a good person, but just keep making bad things happen to me.

School coming up and I gotta get all of them school stuff because he don't wanna help. I just need somebody to tell me this is just part of my journey that is testing me. I just need somebody to tell me I was never supposed to be perfect. I just need somebody to tell me the days I pray for God to see me through the life I'm living.

Life will break you. I don't know, I'm just at the end. I'm tired and I never been so tired in life. I love my kids with everything in me though. There's nothing I wouldn't do for them. There is no life I am trying to live without them. It's OK to be tired—right?

As I write there are so many tears 'cause I know I supposed to be farther than this. I know this was never part of my plan but I know I gotta keep going 'cause I came too far to give up. I just want the bad to end. I just wanna love for once. I just wanna know that it is OK. Thank you much. Have a good night and again thank you.

Is this how much you love the mother of your kids? Are you satisfied with an emotionally stressed, impoverished mother raising the next generation?

This young lady is not alone. She is one of many. If she were married, would she still feel isolated and totally alone? If she were married, would all the responsibilities for the kids fall on her? Would her state of mind improve with a husband? She is overworked, underpaid, depressed, and almost hopeless.

Now, imagine you were one of her children. How could you be normal in an environment like this? Your perspective on the entire world would be bent toward lack and emotionalism, with a "me against the world" attitude.

There is a generational curse at play when each generation repeats the same mistakes as the last generation, and no one seems to break this curse. How do you break a curse? Repent, renounce, and run from it. But if you don't even recognize that there is a curse, it is impossible to break.

Make a U-Turn

Repentance means asking God's forgiveness and turning from the sin we are asking forgiveness for. Renounce the act as sinful and ungodly. Run from that curse, as well as any illicit sexual activity that will open the door to evil spirits. Evil spirits and curses fly around looking for a place to land. Proverbs 26:2 says it like this, "As the bird by wandering, as the swallow by flying, so the curse causeless shall not come" (KJV). Curses are looking for an open door. They don't come unless there is a cause. Illicit sex *will* open this spiritual door.

Evil looks for an appropriate landing strip. Depending on the decisions you make every day, you could be that landing strip. Persistent sin can invite curses into your world as well.

In Genesis 4:7, God told Cain, "If thou doest well, shalt thou not be accepted? and if thou doest not well, sin lieth at the door" (KJV). Generational curses are looking for a place to take up residence. They do not have free access to your world, but you can give them access through your decisions, behaviors, and actions.

The Black community must break the generational curse of fatherlessness and out-of-wedlock births. We must get the father back in the home. Both my boys were born out of wedlock, so I was a part of this curse too. Their mother and I have fought hard to end this curse in our lineage. Thank God we worked through our issues, repented of our sins, and renounced all the curses affecting our family!

We must teach our little girls and boys to marry before engaging in any sexual activity. After marriage, you can engage in as much sex as you want. It's so much fun to plan a wedding and bridal shower, to anticipate the honeymoon, the kids, and the baby shower, and to have your parents pay for it all. Having your parents pay for it all is the best part!

Blessings and prosperity follow obedience, so how much more will a couple be blessed if they follow the godly design for family?

I've heard you cannot test-drive super expensive cars. Those car companies do not want your dirty hands on their steering wheels or your stinky butt on their seats. "Buy it or go home" is their policy. This quote is what we should teach our girls. Because aren't they worth much more than a car?

We should teach boys, "Pay the price of marriage and lifelong commitment or go back to your momma." Unfortunately, boys like to play and go for test-drives. "You cannot afford me" should be every young lady's life principle as she enters the dating world.

In the past, the man had to pay a dowry to the bride's family to prove he was financially worthy, and her parents guaranteed their daughter's virginity at marriage. What if we reverted to that marriage formula? Fathers and mothers would ensure that their daughters were virgins, and grooms would have to have a job, a place to stay, and some money to marry. This plan would revolutionize marriage!

Husbands and wives would be more prepared and more intentional about this new challenge called family. There would be less fatherlessness because grooms would be looking for virgin brides, and parents would protect their daughters' virginity because it would be worth a lot of money. The rule would be, if you want my virgin daughter, get a job, get a place to stay, save some money, and pay me for her! It sounds funny, but it just might work.

This approach to marriage would also upgrade its seriousness, the seriousness of sex and the sanctity of the union. Some people feel that women with a high number of sexual partners prior to marriage have a difficult time bonding with their husbands. If this is true, difficult pair bonding makes for an unfulfilled, unsatisfied woman who is always looking at the grass on the other side of the fence. She is subconsciously seeking something else. There is a fear of missing out. It is called discontentment. Discontentment in marriage is not our goal, so we must try a different approach going forward.

With incurable sexually transmitted infections like HIV/AIDS, hepatitis, and herpes, we all should be very careful whom we have sex with. Is it old-fashioned to ask a person to be responsible with the most intimate part of their body? Is it old-fashioned to ask a man to be cautious whom he impregnates? We are talking about a legacy being created. What makes it so hard for people to resolve in their minds that having children is a big deal?

God's ways have always been higher than ours because He can see farther than us. Isaiah 55:8–9 says it like this: "For my thoughts are not your thoughts, neither are your ways my ways, saith the LORD. For as the heavens are higher than the earth, so are my ways higher than your ways, and my thoughts than your thoughts" (KJV). To be godly requires sacrifice, but sacrifice always brings freedom. So, for every person who tells you that you should be happy, ask your child whether they are happy. Ask your child how it feels to not know who or where his father is.

Several kids that we mentor have no clue who or where their dads are. That is sad. Sacrifice ultimately leads to joy in both the natural and spiritual realms. God's way is the best way to raise a family, and if your pastor or spiritual leader refuses to teach you how God thinks, find a new spiritual leader. Many scientific studies on family have concluded that kids with a mother and father in the home fare the best. So, God's way is the best.

Since He created the first family, He knows what He is doing. He created Adam first because the man is the foundation that holds the structure together. Eve was taken from Adam's rib, so she is beside him as his helpmeet. They cleave to each other in a *holy* union. This union is the perfect scenario to bring children into this world. This union is what God expects. Any diversion from this formula opens us up to spiritual turmoil.

I know marriage does not always work out, but it is worth fighting for! But I believe most divorces can be prevented, if there are two people willing to work through their differences. For the sake of God, the husband, the wife, *and* the children, any marriage is worth fighting for!

There are provisions for divorce, so talk to your spiritual leader about this and consult the Bible and God. But divorce was never God's intention. In addition, divorced mothers often have rights to a portion of their husbands' property and financial resources and may qualify for both alimony and child support. Baby mommas do not have access to alimony, only to child support.

A good book on selecting the right spouse is *Waiting and Dating* by Myles Munroe. It provides a checklist of principles and wisdom on the details of marriage. The book explains how knowledge and understanding can help a person make the right choices in dating and marriage. It highlights red flags and green flags we should look for when selecting mates.

In Hosea 4:6, the Bible says we are destroyed due to lack of knowledge, so having your skill set full is a must when you step out into dating. Most marriages could be saved with just a hint of wisdom. Some marriages would not even occur if wisdom were applied during the dating phase. Both parties could save money, time, and heartache and prevent unwanted children, and, most importantly, they could find the right person more quickly.

What would our communities look like if we selected more compatible marriage partners? What would happen if these unions were not all about lust, infatuation, or premature pregnancies, but about love, trust, honor, duty, and covenant relationship? We would all have mutual respect for the people we were married to, and we would value our spouses as much as our spouses valued us. We would be there for our spouses, and our spouses would be there for us.

Marriage is serious work, and raising a family is even harder. A spiritual shift must take place in the minds and hearts of the people of God. The world is going to do what the world does, but if you claim God, or if you claim to be a Christian, yet live in a way that is anti-Bible, anti-God, or anti-Christ, you are the problem. You are the source of this curse in your community.

I heard someone mentioning crime in Chicago and calling it Chiraq (Chicago + Iraq), but none of the criminals they were talking about came from Iraq. They were Chicagoans. Curses come from sins that have not been repented for in the family tree, and you may be the person who introduced curses into your family.

A godly shift must take place for us to move forward. It will not happen overnight, but mothers and grandmothers, if you are tired of going to see your sons in prison, tired of identifying their bodies in morgues, tired of babysitting your grandkids while their mother goes to school or parties, then you will heed the words of this book. And, more importantly, you will heed the Word of God.

Breaking the Cycle

If you are tired of attending funerals for Black men under the age of 25, you will listen to these words of wisdom. If not, you will discount my conclusions, and the cycle will continue.

Men, if you are tired of being the doormats of society, you will take your place as spiritual leaders of the family and realize that a wife comes before children: "Whoso findeth a wife findeth a good thing, and obtaineth favour of the LORD" (Proverbs 18:22, KJV). If you want the favor of the Lord, you will ask God to help you find the right wife before you start having sex. You will get a chance to cherish her, love her, and honor her *before* the kids come along. The Lord will favor you and help you be the leader He wants you to be.

It is amazing that God has all this family stuff figured out! Yet in our prideful, selfish approach to life, we assume we know best. We don't. God knows best.

If you cannot trust your spiritual leader to lead you in the ways of God, find a real leader who teaches you to read and honor the wisdom of the Bible. Find a leader who models the Bible in his own home. He is disqualified from pastoring if he cannot lead his own family in the ways of God. This statement is confirmed in 1 Timothy 3:4–5: "One that ruleth well his own house, having his children in subjection with all gravity; (For if a man know not how to rule his own house, how shall he take care of the church of God?)" (KJV). A man like that failed to convince the people who know him best that the message he preaches is real.

Don't allow men like this to lead you. They do not have the capacity to lead God's people into the promised land. It does not matter who these men are, how charismatic they are, or how big the church is.

Talent does not matter to God—character and integrity do. Talent can take you places character cannot keep you. Talent is no substitute for godly living and being true to truth.

If God's word is not being taught in church, it is not a church. Instead, it very well may be a social club. This social club will make you feel good and will stroke your ego, but sadly, no conviction takes place. Please don't be deceived by people who can preach the house down but have no personal convictions or discipline.

Social club churches are the main problem in our world—they want you to feel good instead of feeling God. They want to fill the church up with people instead of filling people up with God. They want you to feel emotions instead of conviction. They think entertainment is worship. And they want you to follow them instead of following God.

Sin is very uncomfortable around God. And since church is a godly institution, not a man-made concept, only churches based on God's word will survive.

I compel you to find a place that teaches repentance, baptism in Jesus's name, holiness, and infilling with the Holy Spirit, with signs and wonders following.

God is all wise, so He knows the intent of our hearts. If you attend a church for political reasons, He knows. If you attend a church for prosperity reasons, He knows. If you attend a church for social connections, He knows.

Politics, prosperity, and social clubs cannot solve the problems in this world. Only God can. Many governments have tried to throw policies, money, and social events at our issues to no avail, because the root cause of the problems was never addressed.

If you are concerned about the future of your community and the young men and women whom you mentor, you must fix this. If you are a child of God, you must encourage godliness in your church, school, social circles, and home. Sin will continue to distort our thinking and weaken our resolve about what is right and what is wrong. The modern church has fallen victim to this way of thinking. So, the mighty men must wake up.

The root cause of our problem is complex. It involves the issues I mentioned above, but there are many more that need addressing. We touched on pleasure-seeking men, lack of accountability, lack of emotional understanding, poor government policies, and lack of spiritual leadership. Let's educate ourselves and make changes in these areas.

Ignorance is no excuse to violate the laws of nature and family. It is our responsibility as men to take care of our own. Without protection, our kids are sitting ducks, waiting for a gun to go off.

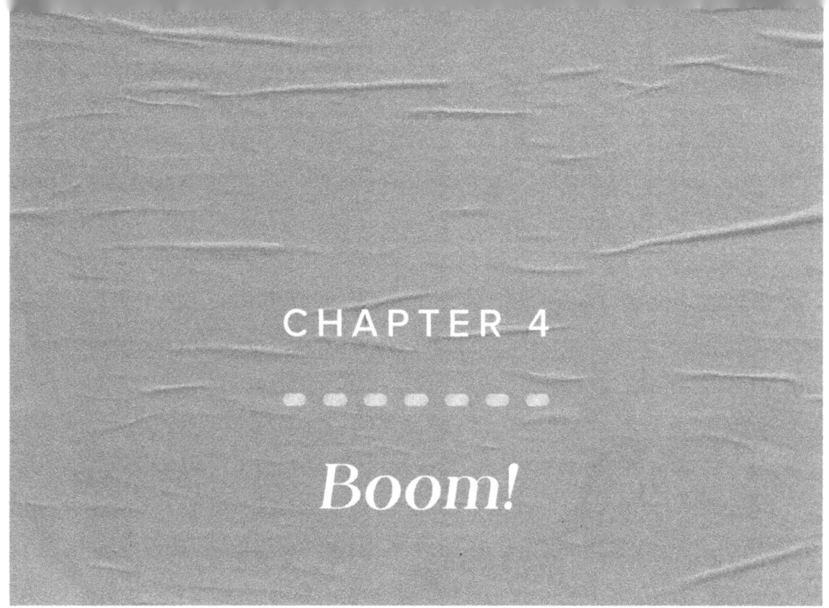

CHAPTER 4

Boom!

It is easier to raise strong kids than to repair broken men.
— Attributed to Frederick Douglass

GROWN BOYS ARE like nuclear warheads waiting to explode. Whom will they destroy next? Fatherlessness has destructive effects on every aspect of society, but modern culture and busyness disguise its pervasiveness. In this chapter, we will peel back the curtain that has hidden these destructive effects and show you the true impact of fatherlessness on our society.

THE BROKEN FAMILY

The greatest struggle for a child is feeling abandonment. I recently saw a 19-year-old young man crying. I asked him what was wrong, and he said he felt lost. His parents were estranged, and his dad had not been very involved in his development as a young man. He shared with me that he felt like he had no one to help him. He said he would be willing to grow in life if he only had a coach, so I agreed to help him.

Now multiply this young man by millions of young men with no fathers, in the setting of poverty, gangs, and project living conditions, and with no concept of God. Can you imagine what happens to these young men? They are broken at best.

Broken homes produce broken kids. Broken homes distort the minds of the next generation, so they believe men are unnecessary to the development of the home.

As a result, modern women have bought into the "independent woman" mentality, and they feel like they do not need men. It is unintelligent to think you do not need the protectors of the home, the providers of the home, the sustainers of the home—especially when the home is the woman's domain. The man brings a necessary but different element to the woman's domain.

God created the woman for the man as his helpmeet. Genesis 2:18 says, "And the LORD God said, it is not good that the man should be alone; I will make him an help meet" (KJV). Yes, women, your Creator made you to complement the man. He did not create the man for the woman.

Broken people have convinced themselves that broken homes are par for the course. It was never God's design to eliminate the nuclear family. In fact, the nuclear family is the most basic element of society. Cement, water, sand, and gravel are the most basic elements of concrete. Without these ingredients, concrete will not set. Hydrogen and oxygen are the most basic elements of water. Without them, water does not exist. Similarly, without all the ingredients of the family, society will fail.

Family is the glue that holds society together! Family is why police officers protect their communities. It's why soldiers give their lives in war. Family is why men work sick and hurt and spend their whole lives to take care of their loved ones. Family is what God intended. Any other model is unbiblical. Anything that will destroy or castigate the God-ordained family is demonic. And yes, homosexual/lesbian relationships fall into the demonic category because you cannot be fruitful and multiply in these relationships. They are in direct opposition to what God desires for relationships and family.

POVERTY

According to Statista.com, in 2021, around 4.8% of married-couple families in the United States lived below the national poverty level.[39] The poverty rate in single-father families was 12%,[40] and the rate for white non-Hispanic single-mother families was 17%.[41] For Black families headed by single mothers, the poverty rate was 29%.

As you can see, single-parent-led families suffer economically, but families led by single Black mothers suffer the most. In 1992, families led by single Black mothers had a 50% poverty rate, which was the highest between 1990 and 2021.[42] We all know Black women suffer the most in America, and they have the worst chances of success compared to white men, white women, and Black men.

So why do I receive so many rebuttals to my conclusions when I talk to people about single-mother families? Why do single mothers get angry when I start quoting statistics about how horribly fatherless children fare in the world compared to children with fathers in the home? Because doing so evaluates their decisions. It takes an objective look at these mothers' lives.

---

39 "Poverty Rate of Married-Couple Families in the United States Who Live Below the Poverty Line From 1990 to 2023," Statista, September 17, 2024, https://www.statista.com/statistics/204962/percentage-of-poor-married-couple-families-in-the-us.

40 "Poverty Rate for Families with a Male Head of Household in the United States from 1990 to 2023," Statista, September 17, 2024, https://www.statista.com/statistics/204990/percentage-of-poor-families-with-a-male-householder-in-the-us.

41 "Percentage of White, Non-Hispanic Families With a Single Mother in the United States Who Live Below the Poverty Level From 1990 To 2023," Statista, September 17, 2024, https://www.statista.com/statistics/205049/percentage-of-poor-white-families-with-a-female-householder-in-the-us.

42 "Poverty Rate of Black Families With a Single Mother in the United States 1990 to 2023,"Statista, September 17, 2024, https://www.statista.com/statistics/205114/percentage-of-poor-black-families-with-a-female-householder-in-the-us.

We could almost end poverty by convincing people to get married before having kids. I believe this model will fare better than the welfare reform of the 1960s. I believe God's plan will perpetually sustain families because it is based on love, not money.

Poverty is not a lack of money. Being broke is a lack of money. I stayed broke in college—I hardly ever had money except during refund check time—but I have never been in poverty. Poverty is a mindset that creates a rut that seems impossible to climb out of.

Poverty statistics are based on income compared to others, but real poverty is all in a person's mind. I had two dollars in my bank account at one time while in college, but I have never felt like it would always be that way. I was broke, yes, but I was just passing through. Single-parent homes have a constant fear of living without. They think there will never be enough, so they must get as much as they can right away, just in case.

In my home when I was a child, there was always enough. My siblings and I never fought over food, but I know of several single-parent homes where the siblings fight over food. As children, my sisters and I felt sustained. We felt secure, and we were content with our shelter, transportation, clothing, and food. There was no lack in any area of our lives. We were not wealthy, though. My dad was a public school teacher, but he made sure we always had enough, because he loved us.

Love goes beyond food and shelter. Love wraps its arms around you and lets you know you are cared for. Love wraps its arms around you and lets you know you will never live without basic needs. Love says you are safe.

Love goes further than a child support check or supervised visits ever could.

Love is our true destiny. We do not find the meaning of life by ourselves alone—we find it with another.
— Thomas Merton, *Love and Living*

TAXPAYER COSTS

Since fatherlessness blows up the financial state of the community, I want to discuss my home state, Mississippi, and how we have suffered financially at the hands of single-parent homes. According to a report from the Mississippi office of the state auditor, approximately 9,800 imprisoned men in the state of Mississippi come from fatherless homes, which is about 50% of the Mississippi prison population. This extrapolates to $181 million spent to incarcerate fatherless men annually.[43]

The same report states that "fatherless girls [in Mississippi] are twice as likely to become teen mothers as their peers with present fathers"—"nearly 2,000 fatherless young women bore children in 2019." According to the report, "Taxpayers [in Mississippi] spent between $51.1 and $57.5 million as a result of fatherless teen mothers in 2019 alone." This same report concludes that "through increased incarceration rates, increased education costs, and other drivers of taxpayer spending, Mississippi taxpayers will see an additional *$700 million* in current and future spending obligations *each year* due to fatherlessness."[44] So, all you taxpayers in Mississippi can see where your tax dollars are going.

I think it is appropriate to tell every child, especially the Black ones, to get married before having kids. It is appropriate to start telling people the truth. Since churches and the government have failed us, the community at large must intervene. Fatherlessness is costing the community at large,

43 Shad White et al., *Dads Matter: the Taxpayer Cost of Fatherlessness,* Mississippi Office of the State Auditor, August 2022, https://www.osa.ms.gov/sites/default/files/2024-08/2022-Fatherlessness%2520Report.pdf.https.

44 White et al., *Dads Matter*, emphasis added.

so it behooves every taxpayer, every leader, and every concerned citizen to get involved. You are paying the cost, so you should at least have a say in the matter!

ROLE REVERSAL

Real fathers make deposits in you through which you can make withdrawals later in life.
— T. D. Jakes

Boys raised by women take on the feminine role and develop atypical emotional characteristics. These boys have difficulty accepting "no." They tend to create excuses for tardiness, missed responsibilities, or failures. These boys gravitate toward the mannerisms of their moms—some even walk like their mothers. I am so glad that I had a dad in the home because he would not let me assume the walk, talk, or thought process of a woman.

I had a clear up-front view of what a man is supposed to do and not do. Men lead out of logic and reason, not emotion. Men give direction and identity to children, but women nurture and teach them. Men raised by women seem to never cut the umbilical cord. They seem to perpetually depend on "surrogate mothers" (girlfriends, wives, boo-thangs) their whole lives. Their understanding of life is "a woman is supposed to take care of me," "a woman is supposed to wash my clothes, cook for me, clean up after me, pick up my nasty clothes, take the trash out, and work." But a man raised with a father in the home clearly understands that a woman should never take care of a well-bodied, healthy man. *Never.* I know several men in our community in their 40s, and they still live with their mothers. That scenario is a perfect example of grown boys.

As a matter of fact, a real man takes care of others. The men at our church care for their parents, their siblings (at times), the widows at church, the fatherless kids in the community, and their own wives and kids. A real man does not need a woman to take care of him.

This is a great litmus test for a real man. Real men can stand alone physically, emotionally, financially, and spiritually. Single ladies, if you find a man like this, marry him. He is ready. He is complete. If a man wants a woman to take care of him or if he is content to live with his mom after age 24 or 25, he is still in boyhood. Let him mature and leave boyhood. Come back in a few years to reevaluate him against a manhood standard.

Real men accept responsibilities without question. Real men have an internal drive that says, "I am built to carry a heavier load than women," "I am built to weather bad storms," "I am built to lead," "I am built to assert myself in every area of life," "I am a man."

Grown boys love for women to take care of them. They take on feminine traits, and they have difficulty making decisions. They also have a difficult time venturing out into the world—there is a fear of leaving the nest.

I left home at 18 and never looked back. I worked three jobs in college and hated asking my dad for money. I decided early on that if I was a real man, I had to fully prove my manhood. Boys who refuse to grow up have difficulty proving their manhood. But if you want to be treated like a man, then you must identify with men.

I am not advocating for a cold, unemotional existence, but I am advocating for an inner fortitude that can handle all the storms of life. It is a jungle out here, and the enemy wants to steal from, kill, and destroy every man. He wants to steal your strength, kill your goals, and destroy your dreams. He has succeeded by stealing the identity of modern men—they are identity-less.

It is easy to manipulate and control people who have no identity. Identity leads to purpose, so if a male cannot identify as a man, he is purposeless. Real men face life with dignity, never backing down from challenges. Real men understand that their passage into manhood must be met with the full assurance of an internal destiny if they want to succeed.

Father absence is so devastating that even girls are confused about their role in society too. Many modern girls/women live as though they are equal to men, and some even approach life in the same way that men do. Role reversal is seen in the comments "I don't need a man" and "I am an independent woman."

What successful society exists without men? What successful military exists without men? What country is led by all women? Who repairs your toilet when it breaks? Who repairs your car when it breaks? Who built the house, apartment, or dorm you are living in now? Men will never be replaced by women. But when a father is absent, young girls have no real standard to shape their minds and hearts to the reality of how male/female dynamics work. There is no Dad there to love Mom.

Several young ladies we have mentored were told by their single mothers to get an education and not depend on men. Well, this would be good advice if men did not exist. But we should learn to depend on each other. My wife needs me, and I need her. We all need each other. Men are so important that God created man first. We are so important that God gave man the instruction to lead.

BLACK LIVES DON'T MATTER

If Black lives really mattered, Black men would marry their own women and take care of their own children in every way. All other cultures of men marry their own women and care for their own kids. Duh? Well, according to Vox.com, 48% of Black women have never been married.[45]

And remember, according to the CDC, 69% of Black kids are born out of wedlock.[46] What is so bad about these women that Black men refuse to marry them? Black men are having sex and kids with these women, so they obviously like something about them. What is so bad about their own children that makes men completely abandon them when they're the most vulnerable? Black lives will never matter until Black men make them matter.

White lives matter because white men marry their women and take care of their kids. If there is a divorce, the women usually remarry to create blended families. One of my business partners (a white gentleman) divorced his wife due to drug use, but he continued to take care of his daughters as if he was not even divorced.

We were going to a business meeting once, and he asked me to go by the bank so he could deposit $1,500 into his ex-wife's account. He apparently did this regularly, and my respect for him went up because he did not play the blame game or the victim game. He recognized that as men, we will have to do some uncomfortable things in life. Handling uncomfortable obligations in life separates the men from the boys. Being able to handle difficult emotions and make good decisions in bad situations says that you are mature.

In my community (Brookhaven, Mississippi), many businesses have been handed down to their owners' children once their patriarchs died. Inheritance is an excellent way to build generational wealth, but if there are no generations, there is no generational wealth. If a man is not concerned about the financial future of his children, his children's lives do not matter.

45 Jonquilyn Hill, "Why the Marriage Rate Is Falling Faster for Some," Vox, February 14, 2024, https://www.vox.com/24072078/marriage-america-race-policy-history.

46 Martin et al., "Births."

I talked to a patient of mine yesterday, who happened to be a Black gentleman with nine kids by several different women. He tried to tell me about their welfare and tried to justify his absence, but he had no clue how his kids were doing. He had no hand in their status or outcome. Poor social wealth leads to poor financial wealth. If a child has no family, that child has no significant financial foundation to operate out of. Each generation must start from ground zero.

The Bible says, "A good man leaveth an inheritance to his children's children" (Proverbs 13:22, KJV). If you are a good man, you will not devour all your resources while you are alive. You will leave something for your children and grandchildren. And you will not behave like this patient of mine who has no investments in his children's financial future.

Black Lives Matter groups fuss about Black lives being eliminated by a racist and unfair system, but what about all the Black lives being eliminated by deadbeat dads? There are millions more lives being destroyed by deadbeat dads than by rogue racist cops.

Groups like Black Lives Matter are a complete farce. Their purpose is to divert our attention to inconsequential factors. There is no epidemic of Black men being killed by white police officers. The article "An Empirical Analysis of Racial Differences in Police Use of Force" by Black Harvard professor Roland G. Fryer Jr. states the following: "On the most extreme use of force—officer-involved shootings—we find no racial differences in either the raw data or when contextual factors are taken into account."[47] So we have been lied to about the "epidemic" of racist cops shooting Black men. It is sad that the media touts these misinformed groups as community activists or civil rights leaders when they are really charlatans who lie and manipulate the emotions of the misinformed.

---

47 Roland G. Fryer, "An Empirical Analysis of Racial Differences in Police Use of Force," *Journal of Political Economy* 127, no. 3 (2019): http://doi.org/10.3386/w22399.

There is no epidemic of racism and prejudice in America; however, there are a few scattered prejudice sects still living in the past. Let them have their 15 minutes of fame because racism and prejudice will never fully die. It will always exist in this world. But it could not stop all the progress we have made as a society. Yes, it hindered progress, but it did not stop it.

We live in a culture where opinion and conjecture are more important than facts. Our culture is quick to view issues through the lens of skin color, but what about other factors? What about the fact that criminals commit crime? What about the fact that police usually show up when there is something wrong? Shallow-minded people inaccurately conclude that all negative interactions between white police officers and Black citizens have racial undertones. All our societal issues are not racially motivated. Some are self-created and self-perpetuated.

Some people try their best to paint America as a racist country, but who signed the Emancipation Proclamation? Who signed the Civil Rights Act? Who fought in the Civil War? These were Caucasian men, with a few exceptions. Yes, racism exists, but it always has, even before America was America. Racism and prejudice exist all over the world, but we Americans seem to think we are special. We are not that special. We have the same vices all other men and women around the world have. The failure of modern America is a failure to fully acknowledge the past and fully teach how prejudice and discrimination are counterproductive to a cohesive and well-functioning society.

Racism and prejudice cannot stop you. This conversation should focus on knowing that these sins of the past cannot stop you. If I can accomplish my goals, despite all stumbling blocks, then I am OK. Condemnation will destroy any nation. On the other hand, America should celebrate its successes and move forward to provide everyone with the opportunity for success. We cannot provide equal outcomes, but we can provide equal opportunity.

Racism and prejudice are matters of the heart, so most of these people will have to change their hearts or die out. However, some people believe modern America is synonymous with 1960s America. This comparison is simply not true. If you are not successful in America, it is *not* because of your skin color. It is because of you. You decided to make the decisions you made. You did not pick your parents, but you are the sum total of all the decisions you made. If you are born in America, you have hit the country lottery. We may not be the best country in the world, but we have the best opportunities. So please, cancel Black Lives Matter because they serve no real purpose in our society.

Fatherless societies seesaw on the brink of extinction. Broken families, poverty, role reversals, and crime are the fruits of a broken society. No one specifically signs up for these fruits, but they exist nevertheless. At the current pace of fatherlessness, America will be the *weakest* of all developed nations because there are no men at the helm.

We should empathize with every fatherless child in our community, and we should also be angry about each time the enemy succeeded in creating a child with no headship. Every male should feel the pressing need to be a man.

So, what do we do to make a difference in our communities? Encourage every child to get married before having children, and stress the joys of marriage. Encourage every child to get an education or trade so that they can take care of their families once they are married. Resolve that the enemy cannot destroy the kids in your community, and become a mentor or role model for them.

Every male can become a man if he takes the right steps! There are specific steps to manhood, so let's explore those steps in the next chapter.

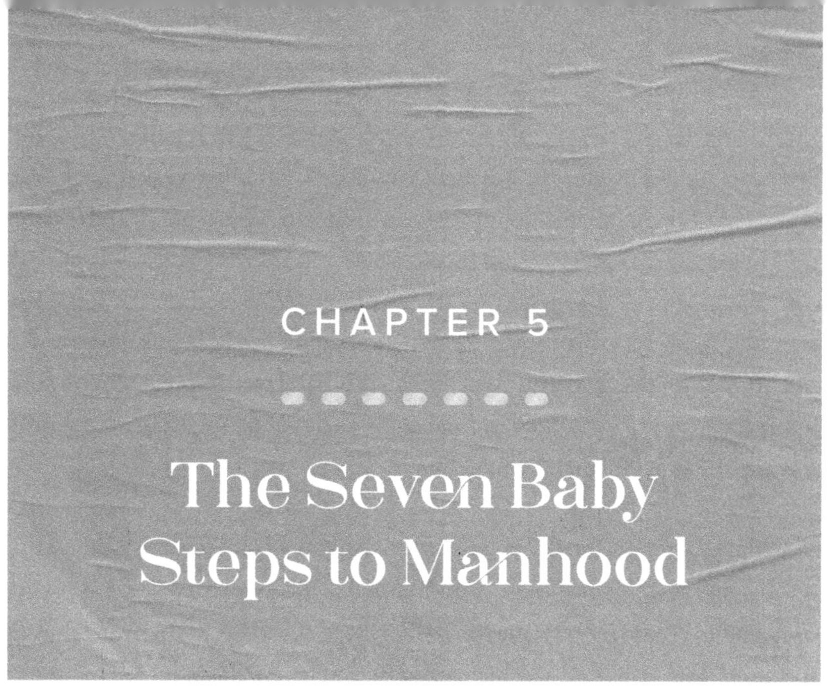

CHAPTER 5

The Seven Baby Steps to Manhood

GROWN BOYS HAVE never been potty-trained on being men. They wear diapers and think athletic prowess is the pathway to manliness. They are more concerned with their jump shots or 40-yard dash times than their manhood.

What makes a male a man? Athleticism? Female conquests? Or something else? The secret to manhood lies in the seven baby steps we will talk about in this chapter:

1. Love God
2. Love yourself
3. Upgrade your appearance
4. Learn to earn
5. Learn money management
6. Mature emotionally
7. Serve by giving back and helping somebody

Loving God is baby step one because God is our Creator, and our identity comes from Him. Baby step two is loving yourself. It is hard to love anyone else if you do not love yourself. Upgrading your appearance is the easy button to improving your self-esteem, appearance, and overall well-being, so that is baby step three.

As a man, you must learn to earn, so having a skill that someone will pay you for is critical to your success. That is baby step four. Once you earn money, you must learn how to manage it well—baby step five—especially if you plan to be financially healthy.

Maturing emotionally is baby step six, and I have to constantly work on this one myself since there is no manual for it. Baby step seven is giving back and becoming a servant. Maturity is seen in a man when he progresses through these steps and reaches a stage in life where life is no longer about him.

These steps will make you a man. Notice that these steps do not depend on whether or not you have a woman. Being a man depends on the journey you take to accomplish what you need to accomplish while you are here on Earth. It is a God-given right for you to complete this adventure. Every male should prioritize mastering all of these steps, and mastery ensures manhood in your life.

You must take the time to learn what you missed, then apply it quickly to life. Join me as we take this journey to manhood.

STEP 1: LOVE GOD

Step one is loving God because love is the most important of all virtues. There are many virtues in life, but love trumps them all. Love is the most important and most basic step in this journey to manhood. If we can love God, we can love ourselves. If we can love ourselves, we can love others.

What does it really mean to love God? Loving God is all about identity. Identity is the basic underlying foundation of who we are. Without identity, a man will accept anything. He will accept cocaine or LSD into his body. He will accept sexual relations with a prostitute. He will accept anything that seems like it will give him purpose and meaning in the world. As the old saying goes, if you don't stand for something, you will fall for anything.

Identity gives a man the strength to stand in the face of adversity. It provides a standard for living, and it leads the way for his ultimate purpose to be realized. Knowing who you are is imperative to a purposeful existence. What you think about is who you are, and your identity is what you dwell on all day long. Proverbs 23:7 says it like this, "For as he thinketh in his heart, so is he" (KJV). When everything fails in life, you can always fall back on your identity. Look in the mirror and ask yourself the question, *Who am I?*

We all came from God, not monkeys. I may look like a monkey, but I did not come from a monkey. Monkeys can't invent, create, or discover because their imagination is driven by survival and instinct. Mankind, on the other hand, can create because we are made in the image of our Creator!

To compare ourselves to animals is silly because animals are just flesh without a spirit or soul. But evolutionists really believe that our ancestry is monkey business. Even textbooks say it is a theory, and that means evolution has never been proven.[48] Yes, animals have life, but they are not living souls.

A living soul has purpose, imagination, vision, and dominion. Understanding our godly origin undergirds your manly purpose, and the appropriate response to a benevolent Creator is love. Scripture says it like

48 Ralph O. Muncaster, *A Skeptic's Search for God: Convincing Evidence for His Existence* (Harvest House Publishers, 2002).

this: "We love Him, because He first loved us" (1 John 4:19, KJV). Loving God is the prerequisite to loving yourself and loving your family.

Without love for God, we cannot fully extend grace, mercy, or love to ourselves or our families. Love means finding the best in people—like God finds the best in us. He is forgiving, so we must be forgiving. Love from God and love for God help us extend love.

How do you love God? Well, my first suggestion is to check out God's love letter to mankind, the Bible. The Bible is just as spiritual as it is practical, and it gives advice on problems we encounter every day. It is a timeless letter that reads you more than you read it. It will help you see what you cannot see and understand what you cannot understand.

Growing in manhood is a process that starts with your relationship with God, and the Bible can provide subtle cues to how you fit in this world as a man. You will never know real manhood until you know the one who created man!

God was always identified by the pronoun He, implying the masculine gender. He is also called Father; and you can't be a father unless you are a male. We live in a world that tries to complicate the truth and confuse the pronouns, but if someone is unsure of their identity, that person doesn't fully know God. It is impossible to know God and simultaneously be confused about your identity! God is not confused to any degree. If He is, we are all in trouble.

The best way to determine your sex and gender is to stand in front of the mirror naked. If you see a penis and testicles, you are male. If you don't, you are female. Determining gender is easy.

I am a medical doctor, and within seconds of delivering a baby, I know whether that child is a male or female. And believe it or not, I can tell you what will happen biologically and physiologically to that baby in about 12 to 14 years. If that child is male, then at 14, he will develop a deep voice and facial hair and will get musty. If the child is female, her breasts will grow, her hips will widen, and she will have her first menstrual cycle. These are set in stone by God Himself and can never be changed.

If you are questioning your gender or sexual orientation, ask God to help you find truth. Truth makes you free from confusion, bondage, and inner turmoil. The Word of God will teach you who you really are and will transform your thinking. God's love letter will eliminate all the ambiguity in your mind and will help you develop love for God and love for what He created.

Modern progressive thought tries to destroy the foundation of what God created. But notice that no matter what tactics are employed, a male's DNA is set in stone. Your DNA is a permanent reminder of who you are and what God intended for all males. So embrace your identity and whom God created you to be.

STEP 2: LOVE YOURSELF

Step two is almost as important as step one. We all have a part of us that wants to be loved, but this starts with self-love. Men who love themselves are easy to love, and they find loving others easy too. However, loving yourself is difficult when you have no identity and no knowledge of the one who created you.

Everyone has value, and I always assumed everyone loved themselves. But I have encountered many people who absolutely hate themselves. They hate their hair, their legs, their butts, their breasts, their arms, their stomachs, and even their faces. They hate everything about themselves.

All the potential of manhood lies inside of you.

What is the breeding ground for self-hatred and low self-worth? *Repeated rejection!* Repeated rejection paves the way for low self-esteem, which can eventually lead to emotional and spiritual ruin.

Loving yourself means loving your hair or lack thereof, loving your fat legs or lack thereof, loving your height, and even loving your weight. Loving yourself means changing the things that need changing, whether for health benefits or personal growth. Other people should not dictate how you view yourself, because your inner mirror is what counts—not theirs. Your inner mirror should always say, "*I am somebody.*"

The underlying themes of your life should be "I am a child of God" and "I know I look good." When I was in high school, I was bullied, called skinny, and called nappy hair, but these words *never* penetrated my subconscious. They never became a part of my story; they never penetrated my spirit or my soul. My beliefs about myself were the contraception to all those negative seeds trying to plant a spirit of self-doubt, low self-image, and negativity. Do not accept negative language spoken to you or over you. Say "thanks but no thanks" to people who cannot see you for who you really are.

When you compare yourself to others, you tell God He made a mistake in creating you. Did God make a mistake? *No*, God does not make mistakes. You are a unique being with unlimited potential, and you are exactly who God wanted you to be.

You are valuable, and if you were the only person on the Earth, you would remain just as valuable. Adam was valuable as long as he stayed in the presence of God. He was alone in the garden of Eden with the animals, birds, trees, rivers, and insects, just being Adam. At that time, he embodied how a man should value himself. Adam named everything, including Eve. Yes, Adam had the responsibility of naming everything. He was valuable.

The Bible warns against comparing ourselves to one another: "They measuring themselves by themselves, and comparing themselves among themselves, are not wise" (2 Corinthians 10:12, KJV). Never compare yourself to others. Compare yourself to Christ. He is our model. He is the ultimate example of a man. He was faithful. He had no fears, no insecurities, and no intimidation. He was complete. He had no inferiority complexes, and He had a clear vision of His own identity and purpose. His identity and purpose cost Him His life. You must love yourself and your vision, if you are willing to die for what you believe in. He did.

Do you love yourself and your purpose as He did? Are your goals worth dying for? We see young Black men dying daily for nothing, so I challenge young men and grown boys everywhere to love that guy you see in the mirror. Do this. Find value in your life's work and purpose. Loving yourself may be challenging when the enemy is attacking your mind. It is not pride to love yourself, because prideful people think they are better than everyone else. People who love themselves are humble and see the reality of their own weaknesses, so they work on themselves.

Loving yourself compels you to be the best version of yourself. If that means hitting the weights, running, or eating vegan for six months to be physically healthy, so be it. If that means going to a counselor to help with emotional instability, so be it.

I know a young mother who is very emotional at times and clearly unsure of herself. She is very talented, but her emotions have limited every aspect of her life. Unresolved emotions will hinder growth in all parts of your life. Loving yourself means taking care of any unresolved emotions.

If you need to pray early in the morning and go on a long fast to disconnect from this world to better connect to God, so be it. If your connection to God is strong, your connection to this world will be weak. If you have a strong connection to this world, your connection to God will be weak. You cannot value yourself highly if you value others' opinions and social media comments more than your own life's goals and interests.

Prayer gives your life meaning and connects you to God. Prayer works on the inner man, and it is one of the best ways to repair the inner deficiencies of the heart. Prayer is the best way to improve the inner man, because the inner man is *you*. So, if you find it challenging to love yourself, try praying and watch what happens.

You matter because you matter to God. So, it's time to find value in yourself and learn to love the person in your mirror!

STEP 3: UPGRADE YOUR APPEARANCE

Did you know that how you look, smell, sound, and feel says a lot about you? Your hygiene either says that you are self-aware or you are oblivious to your personal appearance. Two-year-olds are oblivious to their appearance. Two-year-olds do not care how they look, so what does it mean when an 18-year-old is unconcerned about his looks? It means he is not self-aware and has difficulty finding interest in himself. And if a man is uninterested in himself, he is uninterested in others.

Symptoms of fatherlessness are painfully obvious to the most casual of observers, so my first clue to a fatherless child is unkempt appearance and poor hygiene. We live in a world where some people think that sagging pants and showing skid marks is cool. It's not cool, and the people who do this look like fools without realizing it. Men do not dress like children. Guys who dress like this have no respect for anyone else or themselves. There is a song by General Larry Platt that generated over 452,000 views on YouTube that encapsulates this message about how you look when you sag your pants. The entire song is about how foolish people look when hygiene is a low priority. Look it up.

Grown boys with pants below their waists look like fools, just like the song says. Since when did showing your underwear become a fashion statement? Since men left the home. Since men stopped being the priests of the home. Since every generation had to fend for themselves. Since women started leading in the home. Since men stopped being men.

How you dress tells the world who you are. It tells the world how you really feel about yourself. When I was in high school and college, I would dress as though I was already a doctor. I would imagine myself being in an office or hospital taking care of patients. My inner man dictated my outer dress code. My inner spirit was so strong that it was that spirit, not culture, that decided how I dressed. If you dress like a child, you are a child inside. You never get a second chance to make a first impression, so dress to impress.

"But this is my style," says the immature mind. Styles change like the wind, so please do not get caught up in styles. Bell-bottom pants went out, came back, went out, and are now back. Afros came, went, came again, left again, and soon will be back.

Today, you see a lot of males with hair that looks feminine, and you must look hard to determine whether you're looking at a woman or a man. That's sad. Trust me, I have never been mistaken for a woman. *Never.* There is no ambiguity in my spirit, soul, or body. I am all man. Appearance says a lot about you.

Your appearance should scream, "*I am a man.*" Your appearance should say, "*I am somebody.*" Your appearance should say, "*I am a leader.*"

No one wants a leader who cannot even dress appropriately. No one wants a leader who is so shallow that he is swayed by the fashion of the day. Leaders set the pace—they do not follow the majority. Leaders lead in all things, especially if they are leading families. And you cannot lead from behind!

Dress the part. If you aspire to be a businessman, you should dress like a businessman. If you aspire to be a teacher, you should dress like a teacher. If you aspire to be a veterinarian, you should dress like a veterinarian. If you aspire to be a pilot, you should dress like a pilot. Dress to express who you are, not to express a certain style. "Dress to impress" is what we always say. Dress to build rapport with your customer base. Dress for the job. Dress in a way that shows confidence. Dress modestly. Always dress up, not down. People will respect you and think highly of you, all because you put time and effort into your appearance. And we all want to be respected, don't we? Real men want respect.

Put Some Respect on Your Name

If you want people to respect you, here are a few practical tips to instantly gain more respect.

Hair

Your hair should be short and well combed. It should be worn in a manner that is acceptable in any setting, and it should not offend anyone. If your hair offends, change it. We don't live for others, but we do live *with* others. If my hair kept me from getting a job, I would cut it. As the Bible says, "Doth not even nature itself teach you, that, if a man have long hair, it is a shame unto him?" (1 Corinthians 11:14, KJV). Remember, long hair on men was a symbol of rebellion in the 1960s, and it remains so to this day. Long hair on men is not becoming of a man. How do I know this? Nature teaches us this. Long hair makes men look like women. Nothing on your body should say, "I am a woman." Your hair should say, "I am a man."

We live in a world where satan wants to completely confuse people so that they will never know their true identities, so identity in how you wear your hair should say, "I am confident in the person God made me to be, and I love God enough to show Him off in me." That includes hairstyles. Hair highlights our identity, and a woman's hair is her glory. As the Bible says, "But if a woman have long hair, it is a glory to her: for her hair is given her for a covering" (1 Corinthians 11:15, KJV). These two verses concerning hair in the New Testament specifically relate to how hair coincides with who we are.

Well, you may say, "My hair has nothing to do with my manhood." It has everything to do with your manhood! Your appearance tells the world who you are. Most people look at your face and hair before they look at anything else, so make sure your hair is manly—that is, if you are a man. Regular haircuts are necessary for men. They make you look good and feel good. Hair grooming prepares you for any scenario you may find yourself in. Well-groomed men are held in high regard by everyone. They stand out in a good way. Women also love a well-groomed man.

My goal is to teach boys how to be men—not pseudo-men or semi-men or imitation men, but real men who, when you look at them with one glance, make you say, "Wow, what a man!" When people look at me, they had better say that. When people look at my sons, I know they say it. There should never be any ambiguity about whether a man is a man!

Breath

Your breath should be fresh at all times. You never know when you might be able to steal a kiss. Keep in mind that onions, garlic, and certain other foods can give you bad breath. Smoking can also give you bad breath and poor oral hygiene.

I tried smoking in college to be cool, but I found out quickly that it is not for me. My breath stank, my clothes stank, and my skin even smelled of smoke.

Carry mints, gum, or mouthwash in your pocket or car to freshen your breath. Bad breath can be a deal-breaker at work or church or on dates. People will talk about you and laugh at you if you have bad breath. They will stand at a distance when talking to you, all because of bad breath. This issue costs $1 to solve, so always check to see whether your breath smells.

It is costly to be a man because if you're male, you were born with built-in leadership potential, so everything matters. *Everything*. And everyone expects you to lead, whether they tell you that or not. So pay attention to details because little things mean a lot.

Teeth

Good oral hygiene says you really care about your appearance. Sodas are loaded with sugar and acid, so they can wreak havoc on a smile. I wish I had known this when I was younger. Now, after several implants and much dental work, I have a nice smile. I suggest visiting the dentist every three to six months for teeth cleaning and a checkup. An ounce of prevention is worth a pound of cure. Prevention is best when it comes to teeth, and if you have had a cavity, you know this to be true. Brush your teeth twice a day to keep oral plaque to a minimum. A great smile is an excellent way to get respect and make a good first impression. And remember to *smile*.

Fingernails

Fingernails should always be clean. *Always*. To clean dirty fingernails, pour dishwashing liquid in a bowl of warm water, then soak your fingernails in there for a few minutes. The water softens the nails, and the soap cleans. After soaking, use a manicure set to clean the dirt from under your fingernails.

When in doubt, you can always get a professional manicure. Cleaning your nails is manly. How you clean them is up to you, but a manicure can help! When my wife and I were dating, she would manicure mine for me sometimes, but that stopped after we got married. Go figure! I clean them myself now.

Body Odor

Bad body odor says a person is a toddler in their developmental stage. It says that, even though water and soap are cheap, they choose to live a stinking existence. Water is everywhere, and it costs practically nothing. Soap is inexpensive, so there is no justification for body odor!

During puberty, all kinds of odors creep up, but this is no excuse to smell bad. Some medical conditions can change the way we smell as well, but being musty is inexcusable. If there is no soap and water available, you could try disposable wipes, rubbing alcohol, or sanitizer to freshen up the dark, warm parts of your body. Dark, warm parts of your body smell because bacteria thrive in those areas. In the summer months, taking two or three showers per day is appropriate. In the winter, taking one or two is appropriate.

After showering, deodorant is mandatory. Clinical strength deodorant is recommended if you have high-grade mustiness. Some people are mustier than others, but your neighbor should not be the one to tell you that you are one of them. If you smell something, check to see whether you are musty.

Cologne goes a long way—*if* you are clean. Please do not put on cologne to mask your body odor; it will only make you smell worse. A shower takes five minutes or less if you're pressed for time, so shower if you plan to go anywhere other than the gym. Most gyms have showers, so even if you are homeless, you can get a $10 gym membership for the purpose of taking showers. And you can get in shape too!

Body odor is a true sign of a grown boy. So, if you're ready to leave boyhood and be a man, today is the day to ditch body odor for good.

Clothes

Your clothes reflect you. They speak volumes about how you view yourself. If you dress in black all the time, you may have a black, depressed mind. If you wear clothes with holes in them, you are trying to show something off. If you sag your pants and show your underwear, you are committing a crime—indecent exposure—and you should be arrested.

When I was in college, we dressed up to go to class, and seeing someone in pajamas or ragged clothes was considered laughable. We dressed the part everywhere we went. We did not show our underwear. If you do not have the finances to have a complete wardrobe, buy khakis, stretch pants, and jeans. Khakis can be worn with a polo shirt, or a shirt and tie, or with a sport coat. Khakis are cheap, and they last forever. We mentor impoverished kids, but they dress with class when they come to church. So don't let poor resources define your wardrobe. Be creative. Buy at least two suits, one black and one blue. You can mix and match shirts and ties to create an entire wardrobe.

Shoes

Shoes should say, "I am somebody." Clean your shoes, and wear shoes that fit. Once you wear out a pair of shoes, throw them away.

When I was a child, I had three main pairs of shoes: school shoes, church shoes, and work shoes. As I got older, I figured out there were more categories than three, so my shoe line has expanded. However, three pairs will fit any budget.

Keep it simple and build your own style. If you buy cheap shoes, they will wear out sooner, and they will hurt your feet. When the budget is tight, you may have to compromise in this area, but try your best to buy good shoes. Good quality shoes say you have class.

Women look at shoes to determine if you are cheap. According to HuffPost, "Men's footwear brand Allen Edmonds recently did a survey of 1,000 American men and women, and they found that women judge men's shoes twice as much as men judge women's. 64 percent of women judge a man's fashion sense based on his shoes; 52 percent of women say they judge a man's personality by his shoes; 36 percent say they use shoes to determine a man's financial position; and 54 percent say men's shoes reflect a guy's attention to detail (or lack thereof)."[49] So, trust me when I say that your appearance matters! Even your shoes should say "I am a man."

Accessories

Most men wear accessories to attract unnecessary attention to themselves and because they are insecure. My dad would say that earrings are for girls,

49 Ellie Krupnick and Rebecca Adams, "Guys, Women Are Judging Your Shoes -- Here Are Five Footwear Tips You Need To Know," *Huffington Post*, August 1, 2013, https://www.huffpost.com/entry/men-shoes_n_3689418.

so I have never had an earring in my ear. Earrings are located in the women's section of the store.

The following quote about earrings is from *The Truth Behind Hip-Hop* by G. Craige Lewis: "In the Bible days, earrings were used as symbols of slavery. Slaves were tagged in their ears for identification and ownership. Later, in the Egyptian culture, the mark of two earrings or multiple piercing on a male represented bisexuality and whorish behavior. And all the great kings and leaders of godless civilizations who were lascivious wore them to symbolize sexually immoral behavior."[50]

He goes on to say, "In the early seventies, pimps started wearing one earring in the Black community as a symbol of slavery to sex. It meant that you were a player and enjoyed multiple sex partners. It was called 'macho' from the term 'machismo,' which means 'excessive male or extreme male.' Also one earring meant you were homosexual, depending on which side you wore the earring, mostly determined by which region of the country you were in. This is what the single earring meant and still means: a whorish man or homosexual man. Two earrings on a man was, and, in most cases, still is, a symbol of bisexuality. And now, since our young Black boys are emasculated and becoming very effeminate because of the lack of fathers in the homes, the two earrings are taking their age-old meaning once again."[51]

How does an earring in your ear make you a man? Does it help you earn more money? Does it make you a better husband? Does it help you be a better father? It really undermines your manhood. Something is missing if a young man thinks a diamond earring can replace the void of manliness and self-esteem in his soul.

---

50 G. Craige Lewis, *The Truth Behind Hip-Hop* (Xulon Press, 2009), 124.
51 Lewis, *The Truth Behind Hip-Hop*.

Diamonds are no substitute for personality and character. Diamonds do not create integrity. Diamonds in your ear say you are insecure, irrespective of your age. And most boys wear them to find significance. But really, you are like Peter Pan, because you never want to grow up.

I didn't want to grow up either, and I wish I could go back to being a child fishing, walking through the woods with nothing to do but play. But at some point in my life—and every boy's life—a decision had to be made to put away childish activities.

Our goal here is to redeem the time. Too much time has been lost, and too many boys have been convinced that assimilation equals success. We are creating men, and the lines of demarcation between men and women must be clear.

We live in a day when ambiguity of the gender and sexes is normal, but God's plan for mankind never changes. He always meant for us to look like whom He created us to be. Earrings are inappropriate for boys and men.

I would love to see all males accessorize their minds, not their ears. I would love to see young men accessorize their character and their ambition.

We currently live in a society of disillusioned boys with chips on their shoulders, and their mindsets say, "I have something to prove." When will you prove a point that lasts? Many young men spend money they don't have to buy things they cannot afford to impress people they don't even like, as the saying goes. Is this statement characteristic of the young boys and men you see in your community, or did it describe you when you were young?

Many times young men rely on accessories to flaunt something that is missing: inner strength and security. Insecure people attempt to inflate their own self-worth by flashing jewelry, cars, and similar things. Most times the jewelry is fake, and the car is leased. Material possessions do not give you value. When a person flaunts material things, that means he has attached his self-worth to those objects. Real men attach their value to God.

Your value never ends when it is attached to God. Your value is finite when it is attached to an expensive car or item. It will come to an end. To further drive the point home, I have never seen a U-Haul behind a hearse. A friend of mine in his 80s died several years ago. He had just bought a brand-new Lexus two weeks prior to his death. He drove it maybe twice, but when he died, his daughter drove it away. All his possessions were departed with soon after he died. And no one really remembers anything he accomplished, because he lived his life for himself. He was married and divorced several times, and he lived a life of pleasure and selfishness.

If you are searching for meaning in what you can buy, you will never find it. How many Bentleys can you own? Material possessions are cheap imitators that give men a feeling of superiority and value. And instead of the man owning the object of his affection, that object owns him. Materialism is not synonymous with success. The more materialistic you are, the more unsuccessful you are. Scripture says it like this: "Keep your life free from love of money, and be content with what you have, for he has said, 'I will never leave you nor forsake you'" (Hebrews 13:5, ESV). Contentment and godliness brings happiness and value to your life.

Materialism is vain, and it cannot love you or sustain you. If materialism were the solution to the voids in our hearts, Jesus would have said, "I give everyone $10 million at birth because that is what they lack." He gave us what was lost—communion with God. If your relationship with God is correct, He will prosper you in *His* time.

What legacy do you want to leave? "A good man leaves an inheritance to his children's children," according to Proverbs 13:22 (ESV). But material inheritance is not all that matters—there are also spiritual inheritance, emotional inheritance, and mission-minded inheritance. Fulfillment comes from living according to purpose.

Your children will not remember the new car you gave them, but they will remember the fishing and hunting trips you took them on, the Little League baseball games you coached, the vacations you shared, the nightly prayers you said together, and the church services you took them to. They will remember the deep things you taught them about life. Scripture says, "For a man's life consisteth not in the abundance of the things which he possesseth" (Luke 12:15, KJV). There is more to life than possessions.

Nose rings, tongue rings, and the like are for the insecure souls who need to "feel" important. Any lack of inner virtue or worth exhibits itself in body piercings, nose rings, tongue rings, and so on. Now, many modern people will disagree, but if you dive deeper into the psyche of these people, you will find some voids in their subconscious minds. I have *never* had a piercing or tattoo because I believe God created perfection. He created you perfect too. As a newborn, you were created just as God wanted you to be. You cannot improve on perfection, so embrace what God created.

If God wanted us to have tattoos, He would give us tattoos at birth. In a world of "Fakebook," we need realness in the modern era. If people don't like you the way you are, that is their problem—not yours. My observation of tattoos is that they are usually reminders of bad experiences: breakups, heartbreaks, deaths, divorces, and so on. Why would someone stamp a perpetual reminder of something that incites negative emotions? It brings up the past every time you look at it. And the past is not where we are going. As males, we are leaders, and we are fearfully and wonderfully made. Nothing can substitute for what God has created!

When boys or men want to fit in and assimilate, they will do anything to be accepted.

STEP 4: LEARN TO EARN

Idleness is a gateway to poverty. Adam was working in the garden before Eve was ever created. Adam had a job, and every man after him should have a job. Jesus was a carpenter. If you are disabled, then maybe you could avoid this requirement for manhood. If you are over 18, but not employed, the Lord calls you an infidel (1 Timothy 5:8, KJV). That means you are a heathen. He also says you should starve if you refuse to work (2 Thessalonians 3:10).

Manhood is a journey with a specific destination that any male can travel.

I love the fact that God requires men to work. It gives us an excellent framework to operate out of regarding manhood, and it is easy. Since the beginning of time, laziness has always been frowned upon. During the time of the Old Testament, lazy, rebellious men would be stoned. If we still lived by that rule, many young men would be dead today. All the leeches and bums of society would be eliminated. Productivity is a God-given right.

My grandmother always told us that "an idle mind is the devil's workshop." I never met anyone whose goal was to be impoverished, but I know many people who live in poverty. Characteristics of poverty include fear, poor planning for life, procrastination, and lax standards. Real men build, project, and create their own worlds. Laziness attracts poverty. If you are unhappy with your life, remember that you created it. You cannot choose your parents, but once you are of age, you can build your own life. As a man, you are responsible for your own happiness.

Weak men hate work. Grown boys hate work. A quote by novelist G. Michael Hopf says, "Hard times create strong men, strong men create good times, good times create weak men, and weak men create hard times."[52] The emphasis is not on *what* you do, but rather on *doing something*.

Do something. Plan your life out. When I was 16 years old, I decided that I wanted to be a mechanic, fighter pilot, or doctor. Those were the three career choices I felt would be fun and rewarding. Mechanics' hands get too dirty, so I ruled that choice out at some point. I had filled out an application to the Air Force Academy with a reference from Mississippi state representative Clem Nettles, and I was prepared to submit that application. However, I ultimately decided to go the medical route since helping the sick had a greater pull on my heart. I still love doing mechanic work, and I can spend hours working on old cars. And I still love to fly. Nevertheless, I planned what I wanted for my life, and here I am.

"Would you prefer to be wealthy or poor?" That's an easy answer! Everyone would prefer to be wealthy—and if you would prefer to be poor, something is wrong! But here's the thing: Nobody gets wealthy by accident. It takes intentionality and making the right choices. Below, I have listed some characteristics of wealthy people versus poor people. If you do not want to be poor, just start doing the things in the "wealthy" column, and eventually, your bank account will catch up. This system worked for me and for many other men I know, whether we were Black, Hispanic, or white, young or old. It works.

52 G. Michael Hopf, *Those Who Remain* (Michael G. Hopf, 2016), 18.

Wealthy	Poor
Focus on opportunity	Focus on risks
Invest money/Save to invest	Spend money/Consume
Continue learning throughout life	Stop learning after high school
Admire others' success	Criticize others' success
Take action	Make excuses/Blame others
Have a plan/Leave little to chance	Hope for the best/Rely on luck and chance
Think long term/Delay gratification	Think short term/Seek immediate gratification
Take challenges head-on	Stay in your comfort zone/Play it safe
Make money work for you	Work for money/Make money your goal
Use time wisely/Value your time	Waste time/Procrastinate
Believe in yourself	Believe in fate or luck
Embrace competition	Discourage competition
Be solution oriented	Be problem oriented
Form meaningful relationships and networks	Seek quid pro quo relationships
Nourish a positive attitude/Don't complain	Have a negative attitude/Complain
Be financially literate and disciplined	Be financially illiterate and undisciplined
Set large goals	Set small goals (or don't set goals)
Give freely	Take
Act proactively	React passively

Just like going to the gym one day a month will not make you Mr. America, having a wealth mindset for one day will not change your life, but if you consistently do it for years, you will see growth. Why is all this important?

Women like men who can provide. Women need security and affection, whereas men need respect and sex. When a woman is looking for a husband, she is looking to see whether he can take care of her financially. That means security. She is also checking to see whether he is affectionate toward her and willing to forsake all the other girls out there. So, by practicing the characteristics of wealthy people, you're already halfway there.

STEP 5: LEARN MONEY MANAGEMENT

Did you know that your relationship with money will ultimately determine your financial future? I believe that lack of financial literacy is the biggest downfall of American education.

We teach algebra, geometry, and calculus, but we do not teach kids how to manage their personal economies. I am a nephrologist and do not use higher-level math at all in my profession. However, I use money every day of my life! Money management should be mandatory in our school systems, but instead, we are graduating financial illiterates. Don't be a financial illiterate.

High school graduates today can work the Pythagorean theorem but cannot balance a checkbook. They can solve complex math functions but cannot understand interest rates. Every young man should learn the subtle nuances of income, assets, liabilities, and compound interest and how these financial principles affect his life. It is insane how men work 30 to 40 years to retire with only a fraction of the money they generated over that time frame.

I know several men who are hard workers, punctual, and committed to their jobs. But they do not own any real assets. Assets appreciate in value, but liabilities depreciate in value. So, the man with the most assets wins financially. Boys (grown or not) focus on liabilities, such as toys, cars, clothes, car stereos, and jewelry. But assets, such as real estate, intellectual property, and businesses, should be the focus to gain real wealth.

Debt is also a liability in most cases. Dave Ramsey has a great program, Financial Peace University, that explains how debt keeps people broke. We hosted the Financial Peace class at our church several times, and there are many testimonies from people who have paid off their debts using the strategies taught by the program. Living debt-free is biblical. Proverbs 22:7 says, "The rich ruleth over the poor, and the borrower is servant to the lender" (KJV). So, if you really want to be rich, getting rid of liabilities, especially debt, will be key!

To build generational wealth, you'll need a plan. There is a great conspiracy to milk consumers out of their hard-earned money. The global advertising market is over $670 billion.[53] Why? Because everyone wants your money! So, if you are *only* a consumer, it is hard to build wealth.

It's ideas, not money, that make you wealthy. One idea, the iPhone, made Steve Jobs wealthy. One idea, Microsoft, made Bill Gates wealthy. One idea, Amazon, made Jeff Bezos wealthy. I believe every person has a creation inside of them that could generate wealth. My business partners, Chip Chisolm and Dan Barnes, and I created Corn Xpress, the first corn vending machine. This phase of my life was full of adventure, but we accomplished our goals with that business.

What are you creating in your world? Are you building anything to make the world a better place? In 100 years, will anyone know your name? In 100 years, will anyone know you even existed? What will people say about you and your contributions to this world after you die? We are all charged with bringing value to this world, and the value you bring can get

---

53 "Advertising Market Size, Share, Trends and Forecast by Type and Region, 2025-2033," Imarc, accessed June 25, 2025, https://www.imarcgroup.com/global-advertising-market.

you paid! Below, I created a diagram showing how value leads to financial growth and income.

This diagram explains how we are all connected in some way. Some people think there is a finite amount of money, but that is simply not true. There are enough resources for everyone. Forty years ago, Amazon did not exist, and 70 years ago, Jeff Bezos was not even born. But now Bezos is the third wealthiest man in the world. One idea generated that much wealth for one man! Where did all that money come from? If there were a finite amount of money, Bezos's story would not be possible. Productive people win because they have created value for themselves. We get paid for our value. The more valuable you are, the more you will get paid. And trust me, nothing can stop you from increasing your value.

Wealthy people labor to create systems and to create value for the world, so as their creations are cycled through the world, the consumers eventually pay for the value created. The producers always reap more than was put into the system. But the perpetual consumers are left to fight over the leftovers. They add no value to the system, but they complain the most. I wonder, did Jeff Bezos complain about the current system, or did he completely change the system with the click of a button? We all consume something, but the goal is to produce more than you consume. That is the secret to creating long-lasting value. Please don't get caught complaining and focusing on what you lack. Focus on what you have, and build from there!

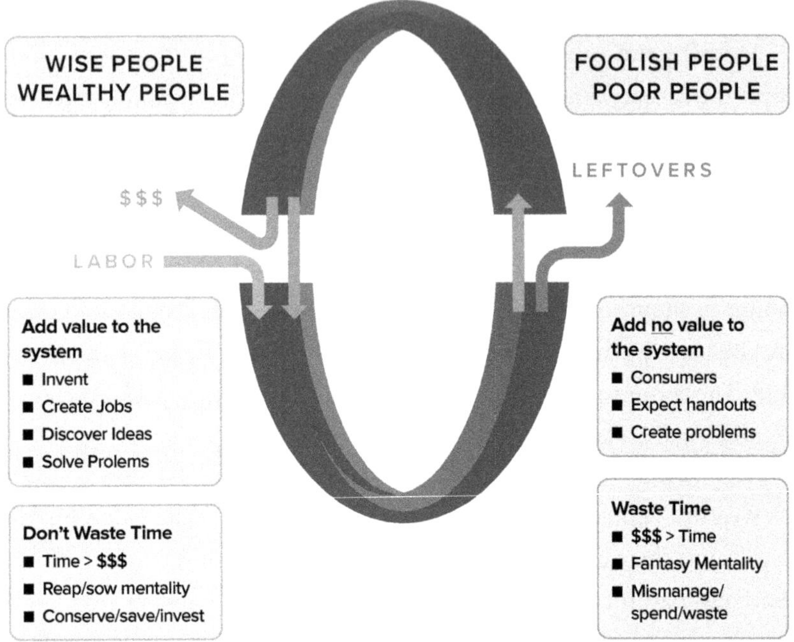

Producer vs. Consumer Diagram

STEP 6: MATURE EMOTIONALLY

This baby step is hard for men because we are not taught how to emote normally. If you ever want to be considered a *real* man, though, you must constantly improve on how you respond to the people, places, and things in your environment.

Your thoughts can determine your emotions, so controlling your thoughts is critical to having command of your emotions. Our soul is made up of our mind, emotions, and will. Our minds (thoughts) control our emotions, and our emotions control our will. These three parts of our soul provide constant feedback to each other, and as Proverbs 23:7 says, "As [a man] thinketh in his heart, so is he" (KJV). Be careful what you think about—our thoughts ultimately determine our destiny.

There are only a few safe places for men to share their deepest feelings and thoughts without incrimination. Most boys are told to grow up but are never given concrete ideas on how to actually do so, so they mature thinking athletic prowess and womanizing prove maturity and manhood. Neither one of these prove anything relative to manhood!

Boys have great difficulty maturing emotionally—hence the title of this book. There is an epidemic of grown boys in the world who mistake age for maturity. They say age ain't nothing but a number. That is true in modern times. Age cannot predict maturity in the modern era. Age should have a strong bearing on the maturity level of a man, but again, age is just a number.

I know grown boys who are over 30 years of age but cannot communicate without using profanity. Grown boys who use profanity as a way of expressing emotion are simpleminded and have poor vocabularies. What's wrong with learning words that can fully convey your message and make you look smart? Profanity is a sign of immaturity, low IQ, and inability to communicate ideas effectively.

The older generation of men (my dad's generation—he was born in 1947) basically told you to "be a man" or "handle your business." These clichés sound good, but what do they really mean? No one knows because the meaning is different for every individual, and the measuring bar is a dynamic phenomenon. Men are doers, and mature introspective conversation is our Achilles' heel. Most men express love by doing, but actions should never replace our words.

Words are powerful; they can give life or death. Proverbs 18:21 says, "Death and life are in the power of the tongue: and they that love it shall eat the fruit thereof" (KJV). Every word you say has the ability to effect change. The old phrase "Sticks and stones may break my bones, but words never hurt" is a lie. Words stay with a person for life!

Words spoken over a child have lasting consequences, so be careful what you say to your kids. Frederick Douglass is said to have said, "It is easier to build strong children than to repair broken men." Words never leave; they are perpetual weapons of mass destruction. Even unspoken words affect the hearts and minds of our children, especially our young men. Watch what you say and how you say it. So, say it well, and say it often. Say it with the intention of creating a man one day.

Communication helps you formulate what you think, and it helps you relate to the people in your world. Express your emotions by putting them into words. Words are just expressed thoughts, so whatever you are thinking, say it clearly. If you cannot say it, write a letter and mail it to the person you want to speak to—even if they live with you.

Words are powerful, so taking time to write a letter is a powerful statement in and of itself. To grow emotionally requires *your* voice. Backing into a hole and pretending you are mute is not an option. If you really want people to respect you as a man, command respect by speaking clearly in all areas of your life. Speak your peace. Speak your mind. Stand up and be accounted for with your voice. Refuse to isolate yourself because you are too immature to express your opinions. Never forfeit an opportunity to express what you are feeling. *Never!*

Seek to understand, but speak to be understood. Communication is how you tell the world who you are, what you are feeling, and what you are thinking. When you open your mouth, you tell us who you are.

Many marriages have ended because of lack of communication. Even after one of my friends had been divorced for several years, he told me,

"I still don't know why we divorced." He says they never discussed the circumstances of the divorce. It was a clear case of miscommunication, or better yet—no communication. That is sad, but we men have been programmed to sulk, walk away, hit the wall, drink, smoke, chase women, or run when trouble arises.

Many men have two emotions: anger and happiness. There are many additional emotions known to man, though, and all males should become familiar with them. There are many emotional wheels available to check your feelings and to help you put your feelings into words. Some people have trouble with putting their feelings into words, but it can be done if you are intentional. Hire a counselor to help you in this area. It will be the best money you will ever spend.

One of my patients died several years ago, and her son was so mad at me and the staff, as if we were directly responsible for his mother's demise. His disappointment and grief were expressed as anger. He fit the classic definition of emotional immaturity. He did not know how to adequately express sadness, grief, or loss. He will eventually be a father one day. How will his kids fare? Incidentally, he is a third-generation fatherless child. He is uneducated, unhealthy, and following the pattern of the stats in this book.

Every male will not matriculate into manhood. This fact is saddening and frustrating because many of these grown boys will be husbands, fathers, businessmen, church leaders, and so on. It worries me that these grown boys will have to lead without the necessary inner fortitude. Some males don't grow up. Some males *won't* grow up. But if you are a male reading this, please refuse to stay in boyhood if you are over 18 years of age. Refuse to occupy the shadows of life because you are too afraid to grow. Refuse to stand by and watch your duty be neglected. Everyone assumes that their age and proximity to manly responsibilities equips them for the job, but nothing can be further from the truth. Baby step six is critical to your success as a man.

Growing into manhood is an evolutionary journey, with the ultimate goal of achieving completeness so that you can serve others. Grown boys are takers. Men are servers. Let's learn how to serve and how to help others, which is a tell-tale sign of manhood.

STEP 7: SERVE BY GIVING BACK AND HELPING SOMEBODY

No man has ever risen to the real stature of spiritual manhood until he has found that it is finer to serve somebody else than it is to serve himself.
— Woodrow Wilson

Matthew 23:11 says, "But he that is greatest among you shall be your servant" (KJV). Whom are you serving?

Most young men serve themselves—this is a classic indicator of a grown boy. Servanthood equals maturity. Servanthood means that you fully understand that your ultimate mission in life is to serve. We are all servants, but some people only serve themselves. Whom should we be serving? God, since He created everything and has the best understanding of our purpose. We should also serve our families in every way.

Men should step out of their comfort zones to serve. While writing this book, I looked back, and I wish I would have served even more when my boys were small. I serve now in different capacities, but servanthood is the path to greatness. Serve somebody.

My mother is a widow, and I have made it a personal mission to serve her in all areas. My sons and I cut her grass, fix the roof, repair the gutters, bushhog the pasture, work the garden, and more. There is no limit when it comes to serving my mom because honoring thy father and mother is a command from the Lord (Exodus 20:12). People who do not honor their parents usually have difficult lives. They never seem to get things right—they struggle in almost every area of their lives. Serving others is about honoring someone else over oneself.

Humility is the secret to serving. God resists the proud, but "giveth grace unto the humble" (James 4:6, KJV). Pride is what prevents you from serving, and prideful men have difficulty saying, "I am sorry." They have difficulty forgiving others, and they find it very difficult to take the lower road. Arguments end with you getting the last word. Last-word guys are grown-boy guys. Remember, servants come to serve—not to rule.

Servants decide to make the kingdom of God better by virtue of their being there. Is your family better because you are there? Is your neighborhood better because of you? Is there less addiction, crime, poverty, homelessness, or fatherlessness because of you? If you cannot answer yes to these questions, you have a problem. *You* are the problem.

You are the reason nothing is improving in your family, neighborhood, and community. You—yes, you. I know this amazes you, but you are part of your community. And you are either adding value to your community or subtracting value. If you left the community, what would your peers say about you? What would your enemies say about you? Would anyone even know you left? Will the dash on your epitaph be the only evidence that you have transitioned this way?

Service is eternal. Serving people is also an easy button to wealth. Everyone wants to be served. As Zig Ziglar said, "You can get everything in life you want if you will just help enough other people get what they want."[54] That means serving people. The greatest places I have served paid nothing—I served because I wanted to serve.

If you only serve yourself, you are selfish, immature, and childish. Babies cry when hungry, wet, or in pain, even if it's 2 in the morning, because they want to be served. They take from their families, communities, and everyone else, but because they are cuddly and cute, we allow it. If you are over 18, you should be serving someone.

When was the last time you cooked a meal for your whole family? When was the last time you washed your mother's car or your sister's car for no pay? When was the last time you mowed a widow's or church member's yard? When was the last time you took food to a sick church member? When was the last time you bought school clothes for a fatherless child? For many, the answer is never, but you can start today. You can start this journey by taking these steps to manhood.

Take *you* off your mind and think of someone else for a change. This mindset will make you a servant. Everyone loves servants. And if you serve, no one can yell at you or say you are not doing right because you are serving. You are volunteering your time, talent, and treasure to be a blessing to others. That is the definition of servanthood: using your time, talent, and treasure to bless others.

Even the Bible says serving and giving is a good thing; Acts 20:35 says, "It is more blessed to give than to receive" (KJV). Giving can open heaven to you and create a free flow of godly resources and ideas. This world lacks ideas. One heavenly idea can make you wealthy.

Giving prepares you and conditions you for greatness. Great people give. Selfish, self-willed, egotistical people use everything they have and

---

54 Zig Ziglar, *Secrets of Closing the Sale* (Berkley, 1984), 22.

spend all their resources on themselves. People who spend it all are looked at as fools, and even God places them in that category: "There is treasure to be desired and oil in the dwelling of the wise; but a foolish man spendeth it up" (Proverbs 21:20, KJV). A foolish man devours his resources so that nothing remains to give. Men like this are classic examples of boys who refuse to grow up. It is not prudent to use all your time, talent, and treasure on enriching yourself.

We were created to be givers, and since men are the leaders of society, we are commanded to lead by giving and serving. If you want to be a leader in this modern world, start giving. You are automatically a leader because you recognize that life is not about you.

TAKE THE JOURNEY (ONE BABY STEP AT A TIME)

Manhood is a journey that every male should embark upon. These seven baby steps will point the way. If you did not have a good role model, let these steps be your model. There really is a solution to all the chaos, confusion, and disillusionment in our world. I charge you to be excited about your inner potential to be a man. Learn these seven steps and work on them simultaneously, then let's see how much you can grow. If you need to go deeper, enroll in our Mighty Men Academy, which is an online manhood course that we offer. We do an on-ground course periodically, so stay tuned for the on-ground course.

Remember, babies crawl, then walk, then run, so don't stay a child too long, and trust the process. Boys who refuse to grow up are awkward looking. Reminder: You have the soul of a champion, and you are the hero in your own saga. Make it interesting. Join the fight to manhood because you can win this one. You may lose every other battle, but you can be the champion in this one. Let's take the leap to manhood.

CHAPTER 6

Take the Leap

My hero is my dad. He gives me surprises sometimes when he comes home from work. And he pays me when I do yard work. And he gave a speech at my school before. And gave us candy. He was a watchdog at Mamie Martin Elementary when I went there. He ate lunch with me when I thought he might not. He spends time with me sometimes. He fixed my go-cart when it was broken. And that's why he's my hero.

— My son Matthew (5th grade) on who his hero is (September 13, 2010)

EVERY DAD SHOULD be his son's hero. Professional athletes and movie stars should never be the object of your son's affections. You should be his knight in shining armor.

If anyone thinks we don't need men in the home anymore, they are gravely mistaken and have bought into one of the greatest lies in history. Fatherlessness is the cancer of modern culture, and it is the underlying cause of most of our societal ills.

The Moynihan Report (which we discussed in chapter 3) cautioned us that the rise in single-mother families was not a harmless lifestyle but would destroy the underlying social unit of society and cause high rates of delinquency, joblessness, school failure, and male alienation. Were Senator Moynihan's predictions true? Absolutely! He saw two futures, and I still see the same two futures today.

A TALE OF TWO FUTURES

The future for grown-boy societies is bleak because it perpetuates fatherlessness and all the long-term consequences of not having dads in the home. A culture full of grown boys is on the brink of extinction because grown boys make horrible men and even worse fathers.

I anticipate that America, if it continues at its current pace of fatherlessness, soon will be the weakest nation in the world. Crime will get worse, prison will be one of the most lucrative investments, mental illness will reach a climax, and poverty will continue. We do not live in a vacuum. We have enough history to predict how social and moral decisions affect the future. Current illegitimacy and divorce rates continue to increase the number of kids being raised without dads. The moral fabric of our nation depends on the stability of the family, so if we continue to assume that men and fathers do not matter, we will lose the battle for a strong nation.

On the other hand, if we overcome fatherlessness, we will lead the world! If we get fathers back into the home, we will no longer be the country with the highest incarceration rates. Since "85% of youth who are currently in prison grew up in a fatherless home," we could almost end youth incarcerations![55]

55 "Thirty-Six Shocking Statistics."

Children from fatherless homes are twice as likely to drop out of school compared to children who have fathers in their lives, so ending fatherlessness will lead to more children graduating from high school.[56] The same article reported that "girls who live in a fatherless home have a 100% higher risk of suffering from obesity than girls who have their father present."[57] Let's end obesity by putting the father back in his rightful place.

The article also reported that teen girls from fatherless homes are four times more likely to become mothers before the age of 20, so if we put fathers back in the home, we could singlehandedly stop teen pregnancy![58] And if you want to end poverty, remember that in 2021, only 10% of children in married-couple families were living in poverty.[59] We could almost end poverty by putting fathers back in their rightful place.

In *Who Killed the American Family*, attorney, antifeminist, and conservative activist Phyllis Schlafly says, "Since the lack of marriage is the primary predictor of poverty, marriage is the best economic justice program in history. We must get the government out of the business of destroying marriage and replacing it with government programs. When marriage is absent, government control and manipulation take its place. Strong marriages defend themselves from government intrusion."[60] These statements sum up the conspiracy to end the family, but they also prove how the family is the best weapon against spiritual, moral, and political failure.

Our future is bright with strong family units because they have a cohesiveness and inner resolve that cannot be broken. As Benjamin Disraeli, 19th-century UK prime minister, put it in his novel *Endymion*, "I have brought myself, by long meditation, to the conviction that a human being with a settled purpose must accomplish it, and that nothing can resist

---

56 "Thirty-Six Shocking Statistics."
57 "Thirty-Six Shocking Statistics."
58 "Thirty-Six Shocking Statistics."
59 "Thirty-Six Shocking Statistics."
60 Phyllis Schlafly, *Who Killed the American Family?* (WND Books, 2014), 206.

a will which will stake even existence upon its fulfillment."[61] No one can resist the will of a people if they are unified under a common theme. The success of our country depends on the success of our families. Pleasure-seeking men are no longer welcome because they are counterproductive to the longevity of the family and this nation.

Can putting fathers back in the home end suicide? As we've discussed previously, "children who live in a single-parent home are more than two times more likely to commit suicide than children in a two-parent home,"[62] and the single greatest predictor of suicide among young men is fatherlessness.[63] We can prevent thousands of young men and women from committing suicide by putting the father back in his rightful place!

If you wanted to essentially wipe out homelessness, then getting the father back in the home would address that too. According to the article we've been discussing, "90% of the youth in the United States who decide to run away from home, or become homeless for any reason, originally come from a fatherless home."[64]

These two futures are clear to me, and these statistics stare us in the face. Look down your street, look in your church, or look in your school to evaluate the accuracy of these statistics. Turn the news on. Go to the projects in your city and make a tally of how many fathers are full-time dads in the home. There is a dichotomy between two societies, and we will reap the consequences of our decisions—no matter which choice we make, good or bad. The impact of the decision to turn grown boys into men is bigger than you can imagine, so let's make men!

---

61 Benjamin Disraeli, *Endymion* (Dawson Brothers, 1880), 124.
62 "Thirty-Six Shocking Statistics."
63 Farrell and Grey, *Boy Crisis.*
64 "Thirty-Six Shocking Statistics."

TIME FOR A WAKE-UP CALL

It is time for the mighty men to wake up! Let's encourage every young male to get married *before* having kids. It is time that we compel every father to take care of his own kids. It is time to convince every man about the joys of marriage and all the blessings that come with it. It is time to encourage men to commit to one woman for life. We must encourage every man who wants to be a father to get married first.

I am tired of the senseless murders every weekend in my city. How many more young men must spend their lives in prison because their fathers did not love them enough to give them identities? How many more young mothers must suffer at the hands of their baby daddies because they are too immature to handle fatherhood? Does the crime have to reach every home before we are compelled to deal with the obvious lack of headship in the home?

Manhood and fatherhood are godly callings. So, let's teach every boy we meet this truth. Family was created by God, and He decided that marriage was the best way to rear children. Anyone who refutes this is anti-God, and yes, that includes the government. America is not the ideal society or model to tell us how a family should operate. The Kingdom of God and God's family system are our model. Men are created leaders, so if we men neglect our God-given authority, we forfeit this godly position.

We should be disgusted at our enemy, satan, who intentionally misinformed us of our roles and intentionally uprooted the primary godly institution—family. Yes, we must make the choice to be men, but maleness is not a choice. It is possible for every man to stand up and be counted as a man so that, when you do become a father, you will not perpetuate this cycle of doom.

Every male should seek God for an understanding of what it takes to be a man. It is not easy—in fact, frankly, it is one of the hardest things a male can do! But it is 100% worth it. As males, let's ask God to open our eyes to the many facets of manhood.

TIME TO COMMIT

Let's commit to resolving all the deficits in our own characters. Commit to being a man before committing to anything else. Commit to helping other young males by fathering and mentoring them. This is manhood, and the Bible states it like this: "Iron sharpeneth iron; so a man sharpeneth the countenance of his friend" (Proverbs 27:17, KJV). It is mandatory for all men to sharpen the character, mind, and understanding of men in training.

As discussed earlier, we men are targets of every known vice because the enemy knows that once you cut the head off, this living, breathing organism called family is dead. If you see destruction, generational poverty, suffering, and selfishness, you know the enemy has been at work. And it all begins and ends with men.

Societies are destroyed at the level of men—weak men make weak societies. Real men sacrifice for their families, just as Jesus sacrificed His life for His family. So, take back what is yours. Take back anything that has been stolen!

If your relationship with your kids or your father has been stolen, take it back. Call your kids and make sure they know your goals and expectations for them. Make sure they know your innermost desires and feelings. Treat your kids like God treats you. They should be given hugs every day. They should be told "I love you" every day. Take them fishing, hunting, bike riding, and so on. Take them on vacation. Spend time with them every single day. Pray with them daily, and teach them God's word.

The traits of manhood are learnable, but it takes courage to discover the missing links. This book outlines the steps to becoming a man, and I believe that these steps can help any boy grow into a man worth respecting. So, tweet these steps, post them, talk about them, teach them. Have discussions about them, and drive the point home that becoming a man is a choice. If you have a penis and testes, you have what it takes to make that choice.

The Bible is an excellent place to start since it teaches you to love God and yourself. The Bible teaches us who we are, regardless of skin color, economic status, parental status, or lot in life. In Psalms 139:14, it teaches us that we are made remarkably and wonderfully! So we have no excuses. None.

Tell every male you know that you have the right to become a man. You have all the raw fundamentals to be a man. Encourage every male you know to learn how to connect emotionally to others, especially his kids, parents, and family.

Make a decision to grow. Manhood is a destination that any male can travel to. The seven baby steps can usher you into manhood. Remember what they are? Love God, love yourself, upgrade your appearance, learn to earn, learn money management, mature emotionally, and serve. These steps should put every male at ease because there is finally a solution to the question of what it takes to be a man.

And despite what people think, a male does not need a woman to be a man. If a male needs a woman to be a man, he is still a child. Let's convince every young male that men can stand alone if necessary. All the potential is trapped inside of every boy, and if he works on these baby steps every day, manhood is not far away. If you want to get a greater understanding of manhood and all the subtle nuances of what it means to be a man, consider enrolling in our Mighty Men Academy (see appendix).

Every boy who wants to be a man can work on these steps simultaneously. Reaching manhood is an accomplishment of a lifetime. What do you want your family to say about you at the end of your life? The comments at your funeral should be comments that would give you joy if you could hear them. The well wishes as you make your transition should allow you to rest in peace because you accepted the challenge of being a man.

What will God say about you? Will God call you a good and faithful servant, or will He call you wicked and slothful? This book highlights the basics of manhood, and it will help any male step closer to manhood. The seven baby steps will give you weaponry to fight the enemy of emasculation, pleasure seeking, irresponsibility, and apathy. These seven baby steps will provide the GPS coordinates to help every sidetracked male get back on the right trajectory to manhood.

So, let me challenge you to put the seven baby steps into action and to spread the word to every young male at school, at church, in your home, and in your community. Give someone hope as a result of your effort to challenge all males to become men.

Let's end the delinquent elephant mindset. Let's stop the excuses and decide to be part of the solution. How should we classify you—as a grown boy or a grown man? Men always accept the challenge of the hour. The only question is, will you accept yours?

Every child has a hole in their heart in the shape of their dad.

— Roland Warren

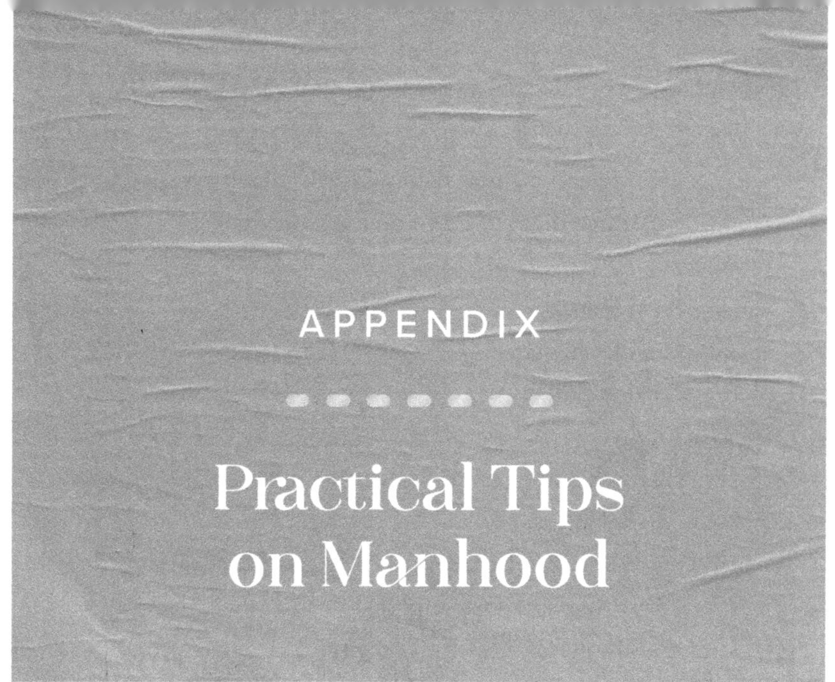

7 BABY STEPS TO BECOMING A MAN

1. Love God.
2. Love yourself.
3. Upgrade your appearance.
4. Learn to earn.
5. Learn money management.
6. Mature emotionally.
7. Serve by giving back and helping somebody.

5 PRACTICAL WAYS TO LOVE A CHILD:

1. Instruction/Direction
    a. Teach them the ways of God.
    b. Read the Bible to them.
    c. Take them to a God-filled church.
    d. Educate them on money, career, and relationships.

   e. Identify and nurture their gifts and talents.
   f. Challenge them to read nonacademic books.
2. Security
   a. Provide food.
   b. Provide shelter.
   c. Provide clothes.
3. Discipline
   a. Establish rules for life, such as the following:
      i. Be honest.
      ii. Understand that sacrifice brings freedom (and therefore work comes before play).
      iii. Do things right the first time.
      iv. Finish what you start.
      v. Avoid idleness ("An idle mind is the devil's workshop").
      vi. Choose friends wisely ("If you play with fire, it will burn you").
   b. Establish rules for the home, such as the following:
      vii. Complete chores.
      viii. Maintain cleanliness.
      ix. Fix what you break.
   c. Establish rules for dating.
4. Encouragement
   a. Encourage their strengths.
   b. Nurture their emotions.
   c. Challenge them to grow.
5. Love and Affection
   a. Spend quality time with them ("Kids spell *love* like this: *T-I-M-E*").
   b. Hug them every night before bed.
   c. Tell them you love them daily.
   d. Be transparent with your flaws and warn them of pitfalls.
   e. Take them on vacation regularly.

Grown Boy	Grown Man
Makes excuses	Owns his actions/Accepts responsibility
Fears commitment	Commits and remains loyal
Focuses on himself	Focuses on service
Acts emotional/Allows the world around him to cause his emotions to fluctuate	Uses his emotions well/Knows that he is in charge of his own happiness
Lives with his parents/Relies on others	Creates his own world/Acts independently
Is unable to resist temptations/Seeks pleasure	Governs himself and resists temptations
Gives in to his impulses	Acts reasonably, logically, and rationally
Is lazy	Is industrious and hardworking
Competes unnecessarily	Is settled and secure in himself
Cannot handle rejection	Accepts life as it comes/Handles "no" reasonably
Brags to cover insecurity	Is secure and confident in himself
Blames others for his actions/Fails to take accountability	Takes accountability/Apologizes when necessary
Struggles with emotional intimacy	Connects emotionally and pursues growth

Acknowledgments

I THANK GOD for the wisdom and strength to write this book.

I also thank my wife, Joy, who loves me despite my imperfections. I am grateful for my sons, Matthew and Jordan, who have all the tools for greatness. My pastor, Bishop David Lambert, and his wife, Debra, have taught us the ways of God. I am forever grateful for them being in our lives.

I thank my father *(deceased)* who taught me how to be a man. And I appreciate my mother's prayers and her endless supply of wisdom. I thank my three sisters (Marian, Kymberle, and Elizabeth) who have given me innumerable fights, as well as an infinite amount of laughter.

I thank our church family, Freedom Church (Brookhaven, MS) who supports me in ministry and in life.

If you are interested in the Mighty Men Academy, please see my YouTube page, @MightyMenAcademy, for details.

www.ingramcontent.com/pod-product-compliance
Ingram Content Group UK Ltd.
Pitfield, Milton Keynes, MK11 3LW, UK
UKHW021913190726
13853UKWH00002B/651

9 798993 972909